T0090848

Set the Captives Free

Experiencing Healing Through Holistic Restoration

Victor D. Marshall

authorHOUSE®

AuthorHouse™ UK Ltd.
1663 Liberty Drive
Bloomington, IN 47403 USA
www.authorhouse.co.uk
Phone: 0800.197.4150

© 2013 Victor D. Marshall. All rights reserved.

No part of this book may be reproduced, stored in a retrieval system, or transmitted by any means without the written permission of the author.

Published by AuthorHouse 12/10/2013

ISBN: 978-1-4918-8429-4 (sc)
ISBN: 978-1-4918-8430-0 (e)

Any people depicted in stock imagery provided by Thinkstock are models, and such images are being used for illustrative purposes only.
Certain stock imagery © Thinkstock.

This book is printed on acid-free paper.

Because of the dynamic nature of the Internet, any web addresses or links contained in this book may have changed since publication and may no longer be valid. The views expressed in this work are solely those of the author and do not necessarily reflect the views of the publisher, and the publisher hereby disclaims any responsibility for them.

The author assumes full responsibility for the accuracy of all facts and quotations as cited in this booklet.

No part of this resource book must be reproduced in any format without author's permission

Unless otherwise noted, all Scripture references are from the King James Version.

Texts credited to NKJV are taken from the New King James Version. Copyright © 1982 by Thomas Nelson, Inc. Used by permission. All rights reserved.

Scripture quotations marked (NIV) are taken from the HOLY BIBLE, NEW INTERNATIONAL VERSION®. NIV ®. Copyright © 1973, 1978, 1984 by International Bible Society. Used by permission of Zondervan. All rights reserved.

Scripture quotations abbreviated AMP are taken from the Amplified® Bible, Copyright © 1954, 1958, 1962, 1964, 1965, 1987 by The Lockman Foundation. Used by permission.(www.Lockman.org)
Scripture quotations abbreviated NLT are taken from the Holy Bible, New Living Translation, Copyright ©1996. Used by permission of Tyndale House Publishers, Inc. Wheaton, Illinois 60189. All rights reserved.

DEDICATED TO

the ministry of intercessory prayer team, namely Joanna, Glen, Faith, Emily, Sophia,
Letitia and my dear and insightful wife, Maria, who work tirelessly with me over the years
in planning the yearly programmes. The encouragement and advice from Grace Walsh,
denominational Health Director in the North of England, has assisted
greatly in propelling the ministry into new territory.

CONTENTS

Introduction

Over the last five years, I have taken a keen interest in the holistic health (emotional, intellectual, physical, social and spiritual) of Christian congregations. Actually, I firmly believe that a congregation's spirituality is critical to fulfilling the purpose for which it exists, that is to say, for the execution and achievement of its mission. Moreover, it is essential that each congregation engages in the central mission, established by Christ when he gave His first disciples, and by extension, His present-day disciples, "Therefore go and make disciples of all nations, baptising them in the name of the Father and of the Son and of the Holy Spirit, and teaching them to obey everything I have commanded you. And surely I am with you always, to the very end of the age" (Mt 28:19-20, NIV).

However, in order for this mission to be accomplished, every congregation must be displaying a measure of health on the various levels: emotional, physical (people's individual health), social and spiritual. Peter Scazzero asserts that "Emotional health and spiritual maturity are inseparable. It is not possible to be spiritually mature while remaining emotionally immature."[1] With this perspective, it is essential that leaders seek to direct their congregations towards being healthy holistically.

Reflecting on the biological body, I notice the parallel between our physical body and the body of Christ, the Church, and in particular, each local congregation. Since all aspects of health are crucial to the body functioning well, so is it with the local congregation. In order for each local congregation to evangelise its neighbourhood and lead people to Christ, its emotional and spiritual health should be improved. It is important to note that the "medical missionary work is the right hand of the gospel. It is necessary to the advancement of the cause of God. As through it men and women are led to see the importance of right habits of living, the saving power of the truth will be made known. Every city is to be entered by workers trained to do medical missionary work. As the right hand of the third angel's message, God's methods of treating disease will open doors for the entrance of present truth."[2]

Although congregations, like the human body, have healing capacities, through the possession of strengths and resources, every congregation lives through a series of births and deaths, and ebbs and flows. So, in light of this understanding, the processes of healing and illness move from challenge to disturbance to regeneration to collapse and back to stability. More importantly, every healthy, growing and effective congregation has eight significant characteristics which can be categorised as **spiritual** (Empowering leadership, Gift-based ministry, passionate spirituality, Inspiring worship services, need-orientated evangelism); **intellectual** (effective structures); and **emotional** and **social** (loving relationships, holistic small groups). Nevertheless, healthy congregations will neither anxiously hurry nor slow down the healing process. The fact that it is a natural journey, healing occurs over time as long as congregations allow their strengths and resources to carry them through their wounded-ness.

It is against this background that the *Set the Captives Free* Resource Guide seeks to outline different types of in-depth and intensive training workshops and restoration seminars for pastoral team members (pastors, elders, bible instructors), lay leaders (such as health, family Life leaders and prayer ministries co-ordinators) in local contemporary Christian congregations in the 21st Century. Pastoral and lay leaders, who (**1**) recognise that their congregations are stagnant; (**2**) observe that the congregation is difficult to lead; or (**3**) recognise instability in interpersonal relationships among the members of their congregation, can make contact for any of the series to be conducted.

In seeking to conduct the workshops, it is suggested that each congregation which desires to be helped in experiencing a spiritually healthy environment, send a team of at least **six (6)** people for training: an elder, **at least three (3)** of the following leaders: the health leader, the family life leader, women's ministries leader, youth leader or prayer ministries co-ordinator and **two (2)** lay members. Congregations which desire to have any of the holistic restoration seminars are advised to assess the congregation's readiness level for this ministry *(***SEE SECTION 3 BELOW**). Additionally, the congregation should complete the Pre—Assessment Questionnaire (**SECTION 11**) and sign up for **Level I** of the training workshop prior to requesting the seminars.

By attending the workshops or seminars you will be exposed to the:

a)Focus: Providing holistic restoration at a personal and congregational level.

b)Mission: To assist pastoral team members and lay leaders in identifying the state of their congregation's health and provide an avenue for congregations to experience healing so that they can proceed to engage effectively in Christ's Great Commission.

c)Vision: Healed and strengthened congregations whose members are nurtured, revived and motivated to become focused disciples of Christ as they use various resources to reach out to their communities.

Having provided this background, *Set the Captives Free* ministry of holistic restoration has been established to provide effective and intentional spiritual care at the individual and congregational levels. This step has been taken seeing that "the overall health of any church or ministry depends primarily on the emotional and spiritual health of its leadership."[3] For this reason, we believe that this ministry is vital so that people who are ministered to in the various worship environments are led to find meaningful experiences with Christ.

Training Implementation Approach

Set the Captives Free Ministry of Holistic Restoration offers training at two (2) levels. The Co-ordinators' training programme is set up for individuals who are interested in emotional & spiritual health and who have a passion for this ministry. It equips them with skills, knowledge and experiences so that they can lead the ministry in a small group or in their local congregations more effectively.

The second level of training equips individuals to become facilitators, who will be qualified to train others to implement the ministry. Training the Trainers' programme is designed also to educate people who want to plan and hold *Set the Captives Free* Holistic Restoration conferences or training workshops in their congregations, district of churches or AREA. The facilitator is responsible for planning the overall programme, teaching co-ordinators, leading programme volunteers, and efficiently organizing and executing the *Set the Captives Free* programmes using the resources and suggestions provided in this Resource Guide.

Brief Overview

Set the Captives Free ministry of holistic restoration aims to provide effective and intentional spiritual care for people who are ministered to in the various worship environments so that they can be led to find meaningful experiences with Christ. Moreover, this ministry was developed out of my various experiences as a member of various pastoral teams over the last twenty (20) years. During this time, I discovered that something was wrong with the congregations where I served as an elder and also some of the ones that I led while being the Pastor. Unfortunately, I had lacked the skills, experience or the knowledge to bring about a change in some of these congregations.

For a long time I have recognised that some of these congregations were unhealthy, but I did not know the reason, neither could I help the people. Since then, I have discovered that unhealthy congregations are difficult to lead (and they often let you know this). Furthermore, they are weak, either because they **(1)** are spiritually mal-nourished and un-nurtured, **(2)** are well nourished spiritually, but are affected by emotional and spiritual parasitical issues which sap the energy, **(3)** lack a focus on mission and ministry or **(4)** are channelling their energies and resources in the wrong direction, thus focusing on non-essentials and petty issues. In fact, when congregations become weak for a protracted period of time, this leads to inactivity in ministry, thus hindering a congregation from fulfilling its mission or achieving its vision.

However, over the years, through formal theological training, intercessory prayer, intense bible study and attending various seminars and training workshops, I have acquired various skills and knowledge which I have put into practice, thus affording me much needed experience to assist congregations in experiencing the power of spiritual care through this restoration ministry. Through these opportunities, I have developed many resources such as seminar presentations, a resource guide and have been hosting a Restoration Seminar Series entitled *A Balm in Gilead*. Additionally, I have facilitated a year-long holistic healing programme entitled *A Journey Towards Total Wholeness* in some of my congregations.

The ministry of holistic restoration has become even more crucial for contemporary congregations in the twenty-first century as leaders and members are aided through spiritual care. This is where Holistic Restoration is pivotal because it provides resources to assist and facilitate the necessary change. Additionally, congregations undergo an intervention strategy in an attempt to experience healing.

This ministry offers seminars on holistic restoration and training for pastoral team members and lay leaders at the local congregational level. This Resource Guide is divided into five (5) Parts: Insights on Holistic Restoration; Foundational Elements of Holistic Restoration, A Balm in Gilead—An Intervention Strategy; The Impact of the Ministry of Holistic Restoration; Training Practicum, Titles and Tools.

In particular, of the many sections that follow below, this Resource Guide provides a theology of healing, a biblical perspective on the ministry of healing and a biblical perspective on restoration in ***Section 1***. It is important to have a grasp of the input of the

Spirit of Prophecy in this vital aspect of every congregation, thus ***Section 2*** shares insights from Ellen G. White by providing a brief survey of her views on how spirituality impacts on the health of a congregation, the relationship between evangelism and spirituality, on the need for restoration of bodily health and by extension, of the need for spiritually healthy congregations. Preparing to Implement the Holistic Restoration Programme is shared in ***Section 3,*** while ***Section 4*** shares the various dimensions of holistic restoration such as emotional healing and intellectual wellness. The impact of ill-health on the life cycle of a congregation is discussed in ***Section 5,*** with the four phases of holistic restoration such as disequilibrium and deliverance are identified in ***Section 6.***

Having provided the theoretical and theological backgrounds to holistic restoration in the previous sections, an intervention strategy is shared in ***Section 7;*** evidence of the impact of the holistic restoration programme on congregations is shared in ***Section 8. Section 9*** provides real cases to be considered during the training programme.

PART A

Insights on Holistic Restoration

"The thief's purpose is to steal and kill and destroy. My purpose is to give them a rich and satisfying life" (Jn 10:10, NLT).

Introduction

The health of a Christian congregation is as vital as the health of the natural body, to the extent that a congregation is equated to being part of the 'body of Christ'. At the outset, I desire to clarify the distinction between the term *church* and the term *congregation*. We would agree that there is only **one church,** which consists of many believers worldwide, meeting together in different ***congregations.*** The church, in its truest sense, is the body of Christ. The Apostle Paul affirmed this theological perspective by asserting that "I am glad when I suffer for you in my body, for I am participating in the sufferings of Christ that continue for his body, the church" (Col 1:24, NLT).

The many congregations which exist globally consist of believers who make up God's ***church.*** With this understanding, we would agree that, just as the natural body becomes sick, so does a congregation of Christian believers. However, " It is not the Creator's purpose that mankind shall be weighed down with a burden of pain, that his activities shall be curtailed by illness, that his strength wane, and his life be cut short by disease."[4]

Part 1: Insights on Holistic Restoration, is divided into three sections. In order to grasp an understanding of God's role in the ministry of holistic restoration, a theological perspective is provided first. Since the health principles adopted by the Seventh-day Adventist Church was due primarily to Ellen G. White's influence, her views on restoration and spirituality are shared secondly. Finally, in order to understand the basic procedures for engaging in the ministry of holistic restoration, the preparatory framework is shared in the last section.

1
A Theological Perspective

Does healing relate only to the human body, or can it be extended to a congregation, which makes up the Church, the Body of Christ? How can holistic restoration assist a congregation in experiencing emotional and spiritual health? How can we bring a theological understanding to the congregation to provide a solution for the many problems that exist? Such questions have plagued many Christian leaders who grapple with a multitude of issues and problems in their congregations.

Individuals who are seeking for a resource to assist themselves or their congregation in experiencing emotional and spiritual health can be helped through the ministry of holistic restoration. Moreover, they can benefit from a biblical understanding of restoration. This section, therefore, provides:

- A Theology of Healing
- A Biblical Perspective on the Ministry of Healing
- A Biblical Perspective on Restoration

It is hoped that this theological perspective will provide insight into the significance of healing and restoration, an experience which God desires for fallen humanity.

A Theology of Healing: New Testament View

The act of touching or symbolic references to it is a prevalent pastoral activity in the Gospel of Mark, with respect to miraculous healing (Mk 1:29-31, 3:10-12; 6:53-56), cleansing (Mk1: 40-43) and raising the dead (Mk 5:41-43). This pastoral activity is portrayed in Mk 5 within the context of suffering and affliction. From this brief background, I will develop a theology of healing from a New Testament perspective.

Jesus, who healed many individuals of their illnesses, raised the dead, cast out demons and cleansed lepers, displayed deep compassion for suffering humanity. With this in mind, He showed compassion for the social outcast (Mk 1:40-44), the hungry (Mk 6:30-34; 8:1-8), and the afflicted (Mk 9:14-29), with the aim of providing "social and spiritual restoration [which] are clearly linked with physical recovery.[5]

It is important to note that since such medical ailments and social difficulties tends to exclude sufferers from their community, we, who provide spiritual, psychological and other facets of care, must seek to provide healing and bring about restoration to the whole man.

The explicit display of Jesus' willingness to relieve individuals of human suffering is revealed dramatically in the episode of the haemorrhaging woman (Mk 5:25-34). Moreover, when individuals are afflicted, their sickness/difficulty tends to deteriorate if they do not experience healing, as it did with the Centurion's servant (Mt 8:5-13), the haemorrhaging woman (Mk 5:26) and the nobleman's son (Jn 4:46-47. Since the affliction is the problem, we need the healing power of God to resolve the health problem.

Miraculous healing implies that power [*dunamis*] emerges from Christ, the Agent of God's power for healing since "He did not ask God to intervene on behalf of the sick, but pronounced healing directly, in speech-acts, that assumed his possession of divine authority to do so."[6] Moreover, our helpless situation, especially in sickness, "highlights the power of Jesus in the miracle of healing."[7] Simultaneously, the recipient is transformed from being sick to being whole, thereby experiencing restoration and receiving salvation. By extension, such a powerful display indicates a transformation from death to life for the hurting, wounded and the sick.

The fact that Jesus allowed power to flow out of him and into the woman (v.30), indicated the restorative nature of his healing ministry which has "marked the coming of the new aeon, the long-awaited era of salvation."[8] Thus, Jesus exhibited this same attitude by restoring the physically afflicted (Mt 8:5-13; Mk 3:1-5), the dead to life (Mk 5:35-43; Lk 7:12-15; Jn 11:1-44) and even the psychologically tormented (Mk 5:1-20). In experiencing the impact from Jesus' ministry of healing, individuals must touch or be touched by Christ, God's agent of healing.

When we consider the views of people in Jesus' era, in relation to the source of sickness, we cannot help but recognise that it is not only based on the medical model, in terms of sickness in people's bodies, but it was "in their social environments and in the larger universe. Thus, healing may require an alleviation of the pressure of one's social relationships, bodily intervention and/or redress of cosmic imbalance.[9] Hence, the act of touching, as a pastoral activity, aids ailing individuals in being made well holistically. Interestingly, wellness includes more than a healthy body. It includes restoration to our human family and the ability to interact with members of our social and spiritual community.[10]

A Biblical Perspective on the Ministry of Healing

The act of healing brings with it peace, restoration and recovery of the whole person. The individual has returned to life completely and can function in the various facets of his/her life namely, the physical, social, intellectual, emotional and spiritual. More importantly, it is God, the Source of all healing power, who restores the human beings to a state of holistic wellness.

A survey of the Scriptures reveal God's role in healing, thereby paving the way for the gifts of healing to prevail from the Old Testament times as in the case of individuals such as Moses, Elisha to the New Testament, with Jesus and the Apostles. After the Fall, Yahweh declared Himself as the Healer, thus assuring Israel of His willingness to care for them by reminding them that "If you diligently heed the voice of the LORD your God and do what is right in His sight, give ear to His commandments and keep all His statutes, I will put none of the diseases on you which I have brought on the Egyptians. For I am the Lord who heals [*rapa*] you" (Ex. 15:26). [11]

The theocracy that existed in the Old Testament era revealed that it was God who pre-eminently engaged in the ministry of healing. Evidence of this emerges when he engaged in mass healing for many of the rebellious children of Israel (Num 21:6-9). Additionally, he healed the defiant King, Jeroboam of the paralysis to his hand (1 Kgs 12.20) and King Hezekiah of his sickness and added years to his life (2 Kings 20:5). Moreover, lepers experienced cleansing (2 Kgs 5.1-14) and the dead were restored to life (1Kgs 17.19; 2 Kgs 4.20,32). As we see people experiencing forgiveness and healing, God reminds us that He heals diseases and (Ps 103.3) and restores the broken-hearted (147.3).

From an Old Testament perspective, God provides emotional and psychological healing; spiritual (Ps 6.2-3; 30.2;41.4); and physical (Isa 30.26). Isaiah reminds us (53.5) that Jesus would suffer, be bruised, and be pierced, in taking our punishment, which would make us whole, thereby giving us inner peace (Shalom) from sin's grip. The stripes and the beatings would provide the ultimate healing, that being, spiritual healing and deliverance from sin (Jer8.22).

Jesus, in preparing for His primary mission, 'saving His people from their sins' (Mt 1:21), engaged in a three-fold ministry, that of preaching, teaching and healing (Mt.4:23-25; 8:16-17;9:35-36; 14:34-36;15:29-31), as he traversed around His community and among his fellowmen.[12] Matthew, the First Evangelist, in describing Jesus' ministry, focused primarily on one aspect, that of healing, through which individuals with diverse types of diseases and illnesses were made well. Tom Shepherd asserts that "the healing ministry of Jesus in Matthew had at least three points of emphases", namely: Messiah-ship, compassion and the necessity for a changed life."[13]

The writer of the Gospel of Mark highlights the pathos of human problems and also demonstrate Jesus' Christological significance as he healed various illnesses such as visual impairment (Mk 8:22-26; 10:46-52), speech and hearing impediments (Mk 7:31-37).[14]

Prior to Jesus leaving Earth, the selected Twelve Disciples had been accompanying Him on many trips and had watched Him engaged in various aspects of ministry. Moreover, Jesus also equipped and empowered seventy disciples to be involved in a healing ministry in the various communities (Lk 10:1-12). These chosen disciples, were empowered to engage in ministry, and obtained first-hand experience by being sent out in groups of twos (Mk. 6:7; Lk 9:1-6) into the communities around them. These individuals were commissioned[15] to engage in a three-fold ministry: preach repentance, exorcise and heal by anointing (Mk.6:12-13). Such a group of ministerial activities was similar to those in which Jesus engaged while travelling through Galilee, Judea and Perea.

Furthermore, at the outpouring of the Holy Spirit on the Day of Pentecost, the Twelve were "all filled with the Holy Spirit" (Acts 2:1-4). The outpouring of the Spirit indicated that God had also bestowed spiritual gifts on the Apostles such as speaking in tongues (Acts 2:4) and healing/miracles (Acts 3:1-10; 5:12-16). The Apostle Paul alerted the Church at Corinth that various spiritual gifts and ministries were given for the good of everyone (1 Cor 12:7) and "to equip God's people to do his work and build up the church, the body of Christ" (Eph 4:12, NLT).

Importantly, gifts of healing fall in this category (1 Cor.:12 9, 28, 30) and no doubt Apostles such as Peter and Paul engaged in healing through the direct act of touching (Acts

3:1-10; 9:10-18;28:7-10). Moreover, Luke, the author of the book of Acts explained that many believers of all walks of life mingled among the community of believers in relation to the episode of Ananias and Sapphira. Furthermore, at the outpouring of the Holy Spirit on the Day of Pentecost, the Twelve were "all filled with the Holy Spirit" (Acts 2:1-4).

Additionally, individuals who knew of sick and ailing people, brought them to receive healing (Acts 5:15). This act enabled sick individuals to experience healing in such a dynamic setting. Luke, the author of Acts, suggests that there were so many people present that the believers laid the people everywhere, with the view that even Peter's shadow could heal them (v.15b).[16] Candida R. Moss asserted that from a biblical perspective, the practice of healing via physical contact is not unprecedented and can also take place with the sick coming into contact with the clothing [or shadow] of a charismatic healer. Such acts, which occurred in the Old Testament (2 Kings 13:14,20-21) and in the New Testament [Jesus and the haemorrhaging woman], can be viewed as "healing via osmosis."[17] This biblical perspective, therefore, indicates that Christian congregations, which make up Christ's Body, God's Church, can experience restoration through the ministry of healing.

A Biblical Perspective of Restoration

Until the Fall of the first human beings, God's creation was intact, to the point that "God saw that it was good" (Gen 1:4a,10b,12b,18b). After God created human beings, they interacted with their environment and the animals, with God having formed the beasts and other animals, He "brought

them to Adam to see what he would call them; and whatever Adam called every living creature, that was its name" (Gen 2:19, AMP). This demonstrated a harmonious relationship between the animals and human beings. Consequently, God relied on His original plan of ensuring that mankind could still experience peace and rest, by engaging in the process of restoration at the emotional, intellectual, social, spiritual and physical levels.

The word 'restore' means to re-establish something to its original state. This is corroborated by [shoob], the most popular Hebrew word for *restore,* which means to return to the starting point. In particular, biblical restoration relates to people in areas such as health, spirituality, social and political structures. It also relates to livestock, and possessions such as finances and property.

In connection with experiencing total wellness for various ailments or difficulties, " 'healing' . . . cannot therefore be focused on the physical body alone, but must comprise restoration to health in the fullest sense."[18] This becomes important since "forms of social and spiritual restoration are clearly linked with physical recovery", knowing that individuals who are affected physically are also impacted upon negatively in their social, emotional and even spiritual facets of their lives.[19]

Individuals such as Sarah (Gen 20:7) and Joseph (Gen 37:22) were subjects of social restoration where there were calls for them to be restored in their family relationships. Additionally, Jehovah counselled Israel to reciprocate [shalam] possessions such as land and livestock to the owners (Ex 21:36;22:1; Lev 24:21)

Furthermore, individuals such as the man with a physically disabled hand (Mk 3:5), the ten lepers (Lk 17:11-19), the infirmed man at the Pool of Bethesda (Jn 5:1-15), and the man with a visual impairment at the Gate Beautiful (Acts 3:1-10), did not only experienced physical restoration, but social restoration. Sickness of various kinds tends to separate individuals from their families and communities, through being hospitalised, being placed in permanent caring institution or being ostracised because of the contagious nature of the illness. When physical healing takes place, individuals are also restored "to status within their families and communities."[20]

2
Insights on the Importance of Emotional Wellbeing and Spiritual Health

Optimal health has been a popular subject of Ellen G. White, co-founder of the Seventh-day Adventist Church. This view can be substantiated through her focus on the topic in at least five (5) of her books, which address different facets of health: emotional, mental, spiritual and physical. Some of these books include: *Mind, Character and Personality I & II, and Counsels on Diets.* The topic was dear to her since she believed that " It is not the Creator's purpose that mankind shall be weighed down with a burden of pain, that his activities shall be curtailed by illness, that his strength wane, and his life be cut short by disease. But all too frequently the laws established by God to govern the life are flagrantly transgressed; sin enters the heart, and man loses sight of his dependence upon God, the Source of life and death."[21]

In light of the vital contribution which Ellen G. White has made in relation to emotional, physical and spiritual health, through her writing in other books such as *Counsels on Health, Medical Ministry, Temperance and Welfare Ministry*, this section provides a brief survey of her views on how spirituality impacts on the health of a congregation, the relationship between evangelism and spirituality, on the need for restoration of bodily health and by extension, of the need for spiritually healthy congregations within the Seventh-day Adventist denominational Church.

Need for Holistic Restoration

- "Every day testifies to the increase of insanity, murder, and suicide. Who can doubt that satanic agencies are at work among men with increasing activity to distract and corrupt the mind, and defile and destroy the body? And while the world is filled with these evils, the gospel is too often presented in so indifferent a manner as to make but little impression upon the consciences or the lives of men. Everywhere there are hearts crying out for something which they have not. They long for a power that will give them mastery over sin, a power that will deliver them from the bondage of evil, a power that will give health and life and peace. Many who once knew the power of God's word have dwelt where there is no recognition of God, and they long for the divine presence. The world needs today what it needed nineteen hundred years ago—a revelation of Christ. A great work of reform is demanded, and it is only through the grace of Christ that the work of restoration, physical, mental, and spiritual, can be accomplished."[22]

- "There are conditions to be observed by all who would preserve health. All should learn what these conditions are. The Lord is not pleased with ignorance in regard to His laws, either natural or spiritual. We are to be workers together with God for the restoration of health to the body as well as to the soul. And we should teach others how to preserve and to recover health. For the sick we should use the remedies which God has provided in nature, and we should point them to Him who alone can restore. It is our work to present the sick and suffering to Christ in the arms of our faith. We should teach them to believe in the Great Healer. We should lay hold on His promise and pray for the manifestation of His power. The very essence of the gospel is restoration, and the Saviour would have us bid the sick, the hopeless, and the afflicted take hold upon His strength."[23]

- "In the ministry of healing the physician is to be a co-worker with Christ. The Saviour ministered to both the soul and the body. The gospel which He taught was a message of spiritual life and of physical restoration. Deliverance from sin and the healing of disease were linked together. The same ministry is committed to the Christian physician. He is to unite with Christ in relieving both the physical and spiritual needs of his fellow men. He is to be to the sick a messenger of mercy, bringing to them a remedy for the diseased body and for the sin-sick soul."[24]

- "The Saviour in His miracles revealed the power that is continually at work in man's behalf, to sustain and to heal him. Through the agencies of nature, God is working, day by day, hour by hour, moment by moment, to keep us alive, to build up and restore us. When any part of the body sustains injury, a healing process is at once begun; nature's agencies are set at work to restore soundness. But the power working through these agencies is the power of God. All life-giving power is from Him. When one recovers from disease, it is God who restores him. Sickness, suffering, and death are work of an antagonistic power. Satan is the destroyer; God is the restorer."[25]

- "There is a work to be done by our churches that few have any idea of . . . . We shall have to give of our means to support laborers in the harvest field, and we shall rejoice in the sheaves gathered in. But while this is right, there is a work, as yet untouched, that must be done. The mission of Christ was to heal the sick, encourage the hopeless, bind up the broken-hearted. This work of restoration is to be carried on among the needy suffering ones of humanity."[26]

Impact of Evangelism on Spirituality

- "Trees that are crowded closely together do not grow healthfully and sturdily. The gardener transplants them that they may have room to develop. A similar work would benefit many of the members of large churches. They need to be placed where their energies will be called forth in active Christian effort. They are losing their spiritual

9

life, becoming dwarfed and inefficient, for want of self-sacrificing labor for others. Transplanted to some missionary field, they would grow strong and vigorous."[27]

- "It is a mystery that there are not hundreds at work where now there is but one. The heavenly universe is astonished at the apathy, the coldness, the listlessness of those who profess to be sons and daughters of God. In the truth there is a living power. Go forth in faith, and proclaim the truth as if you believed it. Let those for whom you labor see that to you it is indeed a living reality. Those who give their lives to Christ-like ministry know the meaning of true happiness. Their interests and their prayers reach far beyond self. They themselves are growing as they try to help others. They become familiar with the largest plans, the most stirring enterprises, and how can they but grow when they place themselves in the divine channel of light and blessing? Such ones receive wisdom from heaven. They become more and more identified with Christ in all His plans. There is no opportunity for spiritual stagnation. Selfish ambition and self-seeking are rebuked by constant contact with the absorbing interests, the elevated aspirations, which belong to high and holy activities."[28]

- "Wherever a church is established, all the members should engage actively in missionary work. They should visit every family in the neighborhood and know their spiritual condition. If professed Christians had engaged in this work from the time when their names were first placed on the church books, there would not now be such widespread unbelief, such depths of iniquity, such unparalleled wickedness, as is seen in the world at the present time. If every church member had sought to enlighten others, thousands upon thousands would today stand with God's commandment-keeping people. And not only in the world do we see the result of the church's neglect to work in Christ's lines. By this neglect a condition of things has been brought into the church that has eclipsed the high and holy interests of the work of God. A spirit of criticism and bitterness has come into the church, and the spiritual discernment of many has been dimmed. Because of this the cause of Christ has suffered great loss. Heavenly intelligences have been waiting to co-operate with human agencies, but we have not discerned their presence."[29]

- "Because the church members have not been properly instructed by those whom God has placed as overseers, many are slothful servants, hiding their talents in the earth and still complaining of the Lord's dealing toward them. They expect to be tended like sick children. This condition of weakness must not continue. Well-organized work must be done in the church, that its members may understand how to impart the light to others and thus strengthen their own faith and increase their knowledge. As they impart that which they have received from God they will be confirmed in the faith. A working church is a living church. We are built up as living stones, and every stone is to emit light. Every Christian is compared to a precious stone that catches the glory of God and reflects it."[30]

- "God has not given His ministers the work of setting the churches right. No sooner is this work done, apparently, than it has to be done over again. Church members that are thus looked after and labored for become religious weaklings. If nine tenths of the effort that has been put forth for those who know the truth had been put forth for those who have never heard the truth, how much greater would have been the advancement made! God has withheld His blessings because His people have not worked in harmony with His directions. It weakens those who know the truth for our ministers to expend on them the time and talent that should be given to the unconverted. In many of our churches in the cities the minister preaches Sabbath after Sabbath, and Sabbath after Sabbath the church members come to the house of God with no words to tell of blessings received because of blessings imparted. They have not worked during the week to carry out the instruction given them on the Sabbath. So long as church members make no effort to give to others the help given them, great spiritual feebleness must result. The greatest help that can be given our people is to teach them to work for God, and to depend on Him, not on the ministers. Let them learn to work as Christ worked. Let them join His army of workers and do faithful service for Him."[31]

Spirituality Impacts Health Positively

- "The view held by some that spirituality is a detriment to health, is the sophistry of Satan. The religion of the Bible is not detrimental to the health of either body or mind. The influence of the Spirit of God is the very best medicine for disease. Heaven is all health; and the more deeply heavenly influences are realized, the more sure will be the recovery of the believing [*person with a disability*].[32] The true principles of Christianity open before all a source of inestimable happiness. Religion is a continual wellspring, from which the Christian can drink at will and never exhaust the fountain."[33]

Spiritual Ill-Health

- "Today a large part of those who compose our congregations are dead in trespasses and sins. They come and go like the door upon its hinges. For years they have complacently listened to the most solemn, soul-stirring truths, but they have not put them in practice. Therefore they are less and less sensible of the preciousness of truth. The stirring testimonies of reproof and warning do not arouse them to repentance. The sweetest melodies that come from God through human lips—justification by faith, and the righteousness of Christ—do not call forth from them a response of love and gratitude."[34]

- "It is those who are not engaged in this unselfish labor who have a sickly experience, and become worn out with struggling, doubting, murmuring, sinning, and repenting, until they lose all sense as to what constitutes genuine religion. They feel that they cannot go back to the world, and so they hang on the skirts of Zion, having petty jealousies, envyings, disappointments, and remorse. They are full of fault finding, and feed upon the mistakes and errors of their brethren. They have only a hopeless, faithless, sunless experience in their religious life."[35]

- "It is a solemn statement that I make to the church, that not one in twenty whose names are registered upon the church books are prepared to close their earthly history, and would be as verily without God and without hope in the world as the common sinner. They are professedly serving God, but they are more earnestly serving mammon. This half-and-half work is a constant denying of Christ, rather than a confessing of Christ. So many have brought into the church their own unsubdued spirit, unrefined; their spiritual taste is perverted by their own immoral, debasing corruptions, symbolizing the world in spirit, in heart, in purpose, confirming themselves in lustful practices, and are full of deception through and through in their professed Christian life."[36]

Reformation Leads to Spiritual Restoration

- "The time has come for a thorough reformation to take place. When this reformation begins, the spirit of prayer will actuate every believer and will banish from the church the spirit of discord and strife. Those who have not been living in Christian fellowship will draw close to one another. One member working in right lines will lead other members to unite with him in making intercession for the revelation of the Holy Spirit. There will be no confusion, because all will be in harmony with the mind of the Spirit. The barriers separating believer from believer will be broken down, and God's servants will speak the same things."[37]

Summary

The survey of Ellen White's views on the spiritual health of the Seventh-day Adventist Church, indicate the need for members and congregation leaders to give more attention to this crucial aspect. The message of revival and reformation was an important topic which she promoted, since it is through this that the spirituality of the members, and by extension, the congregation, improves.

Spiritual progress was needed in her time and is still needed in contemporary times, since the restoration of full health for the body and the soul is God's concern, and should be ours also. In fact, Ellen White noted that the gospel message is about restoration, in that it provides a double focus: physical health and spiritual restoration. Furthermore, God cares about restoring His people to total wellness, a mission in which the Church must engage whole-heartedly.

Importantly, Ellen White firmly believed that evangelistic outreach is the best medicine for any congregation, if it is to maintain sound spiritual health. And, one's salvation is anchored through engaging in sharing the love and sacrifice of Jesus, the Saviour of mankind.

Her advice and insights are pertinent to the theme of holistic restoration, since they are consistent with the practices of Christ, the Apostles and the members of the Early church.

3
Preparing to Implement the Holistic Restoration Programme

In an age when there is immense competition for people's time and attention, every local congregation must still recognise its divine responsibility of proclaiming the Gospel to people in its communities and neighbourhoods. We are reminded that "The church is God's fortress, His city of refuge, which He holds in a revolted world. Any betrayal of the church is treachery to Him who has bought mankind with the blood of His only-begotten Son. From the beginning, faithful souls have constituted the church on earth. In every age the Lord has had His watchmen, who have borne a faithful testimony to the generation in which they lived. These sentinels gave the message of warning; and when they were called to lay off their armor [sic]], others took up the work.

God brought these witnesses into covenant relation with Himself, uniting the church on earth with the church in heaven. He has sent forth His angels to minister to His church, and the gates of hell have not been able to prevail against His people."[38] With this in mind, congregations must seek to provide a conducive environment where individuals are ministered to and are led to Christ. This can be achieved by preparing congregations with ill-health for the ministry of holistic restoration.

Assessing Holistic Restoration Readiness

Leaders who recognise signs of ill-health or spiritual stagnation in their congregations, should seek to prepare the congregation for holistic restoration. It is advisable that this assessment occurs three (3) months before the congregation begins to plan its ministries and programmes. The assessment can take place by:

i. Evaluating the congregation's willingness to request for the ministry of holistic restoration to be conducted. Initially, leaders (pastoral and departmental) need to spend adequate time in intercessory prayer, searching hearts and interceding about the congregation's spiritual state.

ii. Acknowledging that the congregation needs help. When we agree/admit that there is a problem, this provides a positive platform on which to move forward.

iii. Completing the *Pre-Assessment Holistic Restoration Questionnaire* which is in Section 12. This tool will indicate the people's honest attitudes towards the health of the congregation.

After completing the questionnaires, please return them **immediately** to us so that we can analyse them and return the findings to you. By doing this, you will have a better insight into the congregation's general thoughts about its state of health.

Implementation Procedure

It is at this time that you need to select an implementation team of **at least six (6) people** (Refer to **the Introduction** of this Resource Guide**).**

i. The Church Board should select the team and a leader.
ii. The team feedbacks to the Pastor first.
iii. With the Pastor's guidance, implementation team feedbacks to the Church Board.

In selecting the team members, the following is a suggested guide:
- Identify individuals who have a passion for and are interested in the ministry of intercessory prayer.
- Committed to helping the congregation become healthier
- Individuals who understand the dynamics of the congregation
- Individuals who can contribute to the development of the congregation

It is important that you include the implementation of the ministry of holistic restoration in your new plans for the congregation. The reason for this is that the ministry should be started immediately after the plans are in place. The best time I find appropriate for implementing the holistic restoration programme is at the beginning of the year, since the entire programme needs a year for the intervention programmes to take effect. Additionally, the congregation needs time to apply, understand and reflect on the messages and the ideas which are shared and be focused on its healing process.

Depending on how severe the ill-health is, it may be advisable, during the planning session for the new year, to focus more on spiritual programmes such as:

➢ Days of prayer and fasting (monthly & Quarterly)
➢ Weeks of revival, a week of Stewardship Emphasis,
➢ Literature distribution & other forms of street witnessing/outreach,
➢ Special 10—or 21-Days of Prayer & fasting

A congregation which is experiencing serious ill-health should not focus on full-blown evangelistic campaigns. However, it is essential for leaders to agree to the type of ministry programmes which the congregation needs to host. These could be Family Fellowship Days, Community and Health Evangelism Days etc. **Notably, these types of programmes are beneficial and effective in the entire process leading to a congregation becoming healthy again.** This emerges from the planning session during which time all of the leaders will be focusing on the mission and vision for the congregation.

Other Necessary Programmes & Ministries

Apart from the above–mentioned programmes and ministries, each congregation would need to examine itself and select prayerfully the type of ministries and spiritual programmes that would assist in reviving and bring healing to the members. A number of suggested programmes are as follows:

- Re-dedication of buildings
- Re-commitment Service for members to renew their covenant with God
- Year-long *Journey Towards Total Wholeness* Holistic Restoration ministry
- *Balm in Gilead* Restoration Seminar Series
- *Set the Captives Free* Holistic Restoration Conferences which are contained in **SECTION 10** of this Resource Guide.
- Family Therapy/Psychotherapy—This can be effective with congregations which are experiencing interpersonal conflicts or difficulties among families
- *Standing in the Gap* Ministry of Intercessory Prayer—Prayer conferences which can assist the members in being empowered and prepared in order to carry out the Great Commission.

Summary

Christian leaders who intend to carry their congregations through the process of holistic restoration need to ensure that the people are willing to participate. In engaging in the ministry of holistic restoration, one can find it complex and intense. It is for this reason that the above procedures and framework have been provided. As leaders assess the readiness level of the congregation, this will aid them in planning strategically, meaningfully and wisely.

Having assessed the initial thoughts and attitudes within the congregation, implementation is the platform which determines how well the congregation proceeds and experiences holistic restoration. The implementation procedure has been set up to ensure that congregations complete the essential elements of this ministry.

Although the ministry ideas and programmes are not exhausted, they provide a general idea on various resources that can be used to assist a congregation in experiencing emotional and spiritual wellness.

PART B

Foundational Elements of Holistic Restoration

"The Spirit of the Lord *is* upon Me, Because He has anointed Me To preach the gospel to *the* poor; He has sent Me to heal the brokenhearted, To proclaim liberty to *the* captives" (Lk 4:18, NKJV).

Introduction

The need for holistic restoration is grounded in the fact that each of us is an emotional, intellectual, social, spiritual and physical being. There is no greater desire of God than to restore His people to the original spiritual state. The idea of restoration implies returning something that was removed or returning something to its former and better condition. The human race has been robbed of its emotional intellectual, physical, social and spiritual well-being. However, God has promised full restoration, some of which can be experienced in this present life. Importantly, Jesus reminded us in John 10:10 that "I have come that they may have life, and that they may have it more abundantly" (NKJV). Moreover, we will experience complete restoration in the new earth and new heaven.

It is the **Foundational Elements of Holistic Restoration** that sets the stage for providing holistic restoration in order for you to experience the level of well-being necessary for you and your congregation to minister through God's power and by His grace. Although God made mankind with total and holistic well-being, the entrance of sin has impacted negatively on our well-being, thus bringing about disharmony among us and disease in our bodies.

PART B: Foundational Elements of Holistic Restoration, seeks to create the basis for this ministry by sharing aspects of the five-dimensional perspective of holistic restoration, namely emotional, physical, intellectual, social and spiritual elements. Since a Christian congregation is perceived as a living organism, with a life cycle, it is likely that it will experience ill-health. It is here that the life cycle of a congregation will be examined and how its health can be impacted upon.

Many individuals who experience some form of ill-health immediately seek for restoration and healing. However, there are four (4) phases we need to go through prior to experiencing healing, be it on an individual or congregational level, hence the reason for the examination of the phases of holistic restoration.

It is hoped that as you reflect on the information in these sections and engage in the activities, that you will grasp an understanding of the need for this ministry personally and corporately.

4
Five-Dimensional Perspective of Holistic Restoration

Since Jesus came "to heal the broken-hearted, to proclaim liberty to the captives and recovery of sight to the blind and to set at liberty those that are oppressed" Luke 4:16, NKJV), we should seek to experience such restoration through the power of prayer and healing. Holistic restoration, however, starts with repentance, a spiritual act of turning our hearts back to God with fasting, prayer and weeping (Joel 2:12-17). Moreover, we are required to sanctify or set ourselves apart for holy use so that God may renew us spiritually. In order to experience this desired restoration, the following resources can be used:

- Emotional Healing
- Intellectual Wellness
- Social Restoration
- Spiritual Restoration
- Physical Healing

Emotional Healing

Some of us may have been hurt, may have been disappointed by someone, rejected, abandoned, abused or even bruised. Our wounds may not have been healed and we are still angry and seeking forgiveness. The good news is that we do not have to live with such unhealed wounds forever because Christ is willing to heal our

wounds. Often times, we have to take responsibility for our own healing by coming to God in prayer and expose ourselves to Him.

In order to experience emotional healing, it is important that we remember God's promise in Psalm 147:3 which reminds us that "He heals the brokenhearted and binds up their wounds." Moreover, Jesus came "to proclaim liberty to the captives, to set at liberty those who are oppressed" (Luke 4:18). This is an indication that our emotional well-being is important to God.

TASK—Read Philippians 3:7

Meditate/Reflect on the text and WRITE down any insights/ideas that comes to your mind.

Identify the message you have gained from the text or the information you have acquired. (Don't be afraid to mention it)

Ask the question: Why should I have to **give up** the things I fancy holding on to?

Revert to Acts 8:1-4, Phil. 3:4-6. How profitable was Paul's background to him as a Christian? What benefit are your **painful events** to you?

APPLY: In Philippians 3:7, the word *count* means to consider, regard. The word *loss* means worthless. Are there any situations that you believe are not worth holding onto?

Suggested Guidelines for Using the information Below

The issues in your life at **present** are not pleasant. They have been very painful. By the grace of God and the power of the **Holy Spirit,** you can move beyond your present condition.

♦ Describe what you are aware of, what you have discovered or found out.
  For example, are there un-Christlike behaviour or selfishness etc?
  (I walk alongside you even now and do realise that this is a painful moment. I want to encourage you to take a radical approach:

♦ Talk to God about the situation by telling him exactly how you **feel.**
  How do you **honestly** feel about the situation?
  Pour out your heart to God. **Be opened** as much as possible. **Share** your emotions with the Lord. Do you feel bitter or angry? Do you think it is fair?

  (I am aware that you are in God's presence, but brokenness transcends or cuts across formalities.)

♦ Be radical enough **to ask questions** as you talk to Him.

  MAJOR QUESTIONS

  Lord, what are you saying to me through this situation?
  Why did it happen? Why did you allow it to happen?
  Why are you allowing/ Why did you allow this situation to occur?
  Lord, what do you want me to do about this situation?

For your own spiritual development and progress, you need to consider if the things you have discovered (are aware of) are worth focusing on or are worth your attention.

Prayer Session: Pray along these lines, but according to where you are in this situation at the moment. **Ask the Lord to flush you, wash your mind, and clear your thoughts. Ask the Lord for the power to see those things, which you are aware of, as worthless. Pray for a new perspective of the entire situation.**

Intellectual Wellness

Mankind was made with an intellectual capacity so that he/she can think, reason, discuss and share ideas on a cognitive level. Thus, we have been blessed with a mind, the seat of consciousness, thought and feelings. Moreover, it is the area where concentration takes place and where our intellectual powers lie. It is therefore, important to note that our "thoughts help define which mood we experience in a given situation. Once a mood is present, it is accompanied by additional thoughts that support and strengthen the mood."[39] This perspective indicates that our thoughts contribute to the type of mood we experience, be it anger, sadness or nervousness.

Scripture, therefore, advises: "Do not conform any longer to the pattern of this world, but be transformed by the renewing of your mind. Then you will be able to test and approve what God's will is— his good, pleasing and perfect will" (Rom 12:2, NIV).

Since this is an essential perspective that can impact on our entire being and on how we function, I believe that this can also be extended to every Christian congregation. The thoughts which prevail among the members creates an impact on the mood which exists in the sanctuary weekly. Thus, positive thinking such as "I like to be with the members and appreciate my congregation can create a happy mood. Similarly, negative thinking such as "this congregation is so boring and dead", if adopted by some of the members, can impact on others and lead them into adopting a mood that can be destructive to the ministry in the congregation.

Another impact which our thoughts have is on our actions. For example, if we begin to think about an individual and develop a hateful attitude towards that person, this could lead to us avoiding them whenever we see them, especially in a shopping centre or in a park. When we become angry with someone, we experience the tendency to strike them or engage in a fight.

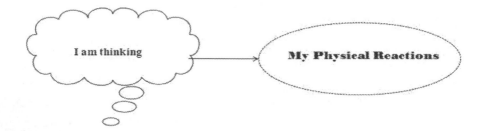

Apart from the above, our environment can have an impact on our thoughts. From a church perspective, if the worship session is uninspiring and the delivery of the sermon is lifeless on a weekly basis, this could lead you to conclude that Christianity is boring and dead. Such thoughts can then lead you to develop particular negative moods, thus causing you to respond inappropriately to all that is taking place in your congregation. It is important to note that "Beliefs can be influenced by your cultural/ethnic background, gender, neighbourhood, family beliefs and practices, religion and the media."[40] These social, cultural and religious environments assist in developing us and therefore, contribute to the types of thoughts we tend to produce generally.

On a intellectual level we create an impact on church members and by extension, the entire congregation. However, in order for our congregations to minister to individuals powerfully and effectively, the members must produce the type of thinking which inspires and motivates each other to engage in ministry. Unless the Holy Spirit, through intercessory prayer, cleans our thoughts and aid us in developing positive thoughts, the congregation could find it difficult to move ahead and therefore, could stagnate.

The following texts also indicate the need for intellectual soundness:

> ➤ Let this same attitude and purpose and [humble] mind be in you which was in Christ Jesus: [Let Him be your example in humility:] ;Who, although being essentially one with God and in the form of God [[a]possessing the fullness of the attributes which make God God], did not [b]think this equality with God was a thing to be eagerly grasped [c]or retained, But stripped Himself [of all privileges and [d]rightful dignity], so as to assume the guise of a servant (slave), in that He became like men and was born a human being.
> ### *(Phillippians 2:5-7, AMP)*

> ➤ For God did not give us a spirit of timidity (of cowardice, of craven and cringing and fawning fear), but [He has given us a spirit] of power and of love and of calm and well-balanced mind and discipline and self-control.
> ### *(2 Tim 1:7, AMP)*

Social Restoration

Since the Fall in the Garden of Eden, where the relationship between God and the first human beings became strained, mankind has been having difficulty in experiencing social wellness. This is demonstrated in various ways such as coveting each other possessions, injuring each other and being unable to get along with other people. Christ, in seeking to assist us in experiencing social wellness, commanded us to " . . . love the Lord your God with all your heart, with all your soul, with all your mind, and with all your strength.' This *is* the first commandment. And the second, like *it, is* this: 'You shall love your neighbor as yourself.' There is no other commandment greater than these" (St. Mark 12:30-31, NKJV).

Such a command seems fitting, knowing that the human race has moved away from God because of sin and no longer craves for the divine presence on our own.

> **Social wellness** can be viewed as the ability to interact effectively with each other and to develop meaningful relationships that can impact one's quality of life.

When we apply this perspective to our congregations, we can ask the question: To what extent do the members in your congregation form meaningful relationships with each other? Social interaction is vital to the functioning of a congregation, since each member is part of the body of Christ and therefore, each member should be in harmony so that the particular congregation can be effective. In his Christological prayer, Jesus pleaded with His Father, by noting that "I do not pray for these alone, but also for those who will[a] believe in Me through their word; that they all may be one, as You, Father, *are* in Me, and I in You; that they also may be one in Us, that the world may believe that You sent Me" (Jn 17:20-21, NKJV). From this prayer, it is Jesus' desire for each of us to appreciate each other's company, interact and socialise meaningfully. However, unity emerges out of earnest intercessory prayer and the impact of the Holy spirit on our lives and throughout a congregation. Social restoration, therefore, seeks to create positive loving relationships among members and also positively impacts on more members becoming involved in the life of the congregation.

A number of biblical references which indicates God's desire for us to have social wellness are:

➢ By this all will know that you are My disciples, if you have love for one another *(Jn 13:35, NKJV).*
➢ Bear one another's burdens, and so fulfill the law of Christ *(Gal 6:2, NKJV).*

Spiritual Revival/Renewal

The Christian journey has various struggles with which individuals have being affected spiritually. David, during his spiritual difficulty, pleaded with God for him to restore the joy of salvation to him (Psalm 51:12, NKJV). The implication is that sin takes away the divine joy and brings guilt and pain.

When we repent and allow God to revive us, there is rejoicing in heaven and God promises to give blessings of wine, oil and grain along with peace (Joel 2:18-20, NKJV). Such a divine renewal also brings a message of hope, there is happiness and joy in our hearts and various aspects of our lives will flourish (Joel 2:21-24, NKJV).

By interceding to God during our spiritual downturn, we can experience spiritual restoration. Interestingly, the prophet Joel reminded us that God "will restore to you the years that the swarming locust has eaten" (2:25, NKJV).

> This will culminate in a spiritual awakening when God will empower us with His Spirit.

This will culminate in a spiritual awakening when God will empower us with His Spirit (Joel 2:28-32). The Psalmist echoed hearty sentiments by making us aware that God "restores my soul" (Psalm 23:3). Such a work refreshes the soul and inspires the heart so that we can be in tune with God.

Other examples of spiritual healing are:

➢ A plea for a troubled soul *(Psalm 6:2-3).*
➢ A prayer of repentance for a troubled soul (*Psalm 41:4).*

Physical Healing

Many individuals today are afflicted with various physical illnesses and ailments, some of which medical science are unable to discover appropriate cures. Diseases such as AIDS, strokes, cancers and mental instability have been destroying the human body. It is important to acknowledge our sickness, but from a biblical perspective, we do not have to accept our ailments since John wrote "I pray that you may enjoy good health and that all may go well with you, even as your soul is getting along well" (3 John 2).

The Scriptures alert us of God's willingness to provide physical healing when He declared "If you diligently heed the voice of the LORD your God and do what is right in His sight, give ear to His commandments and keep all His statutes, I will put none of the diseases on you which I have brought on the Egyptians. For I *am* the LORD who heals you" (Exodus 15:26).

Moreover, the disciples were commissioned in Mark 6:12-13 to engage in a three-fold ministry of preaching the message of repentance, exorcising demons and healing by anointing. Jesus also reminded the disciples of their primary task, that of preaching the Gospel (Mark 16:15).

> **Moreover, the disciples were commissioned in Mark 6:12-13 to engage in a three-fold ministry of preaching repentance, exorcising demons and healing by anointing.**

However, Christ anticipated that other people will believe on Him through the disciples' message. Hence, Jesus outlined four signs that would accompany those who believe in Him, one of which is healing by laying on of hands. This pronouncement was also advocated and expanded in James 5:13-16. Other biblical references exist, indicating God's intentions for our physical well-being:

➤ An awareness that God heals our diseases.
   (Psalm 30:2; 103:3)

➤ A promise to restore health by healing our wounds.
   (Isaiah 30:26; Jeremiah 8:22; 30:17)

Summary

From a biblical perspective, our emotional, intellectual, physical, social and spiritual well-being are important to God. Scripture reveals that we have a responsibility towards our restoration in these various areas of our congregations. Importantly, when each of these areas is Christ-directed, we are able to focus and give God the honour and praise that belongs to Him. This is where prayer becomes pivotal, central and significant to our spiritual growth and development. Our prayer allows us to talk with God about these areas of our lives so that He may bring about the appropriate changes according to His will. May we experience true holistic restoration as we dedicate and re-commit ourselves to Jesus, our Saviour and Redeemer.

5
Ill-Health and A Congregation's Life Cycle

We are reminded that "The church is God's appointed agency for the salvation of men. It was organized for service, and its mission is to carry the gospel to the world. From the beginning it has been God's plan that through His church shall be reflected to the world His fullness and His sufficiency. The members of the church, those whom He has called out of darkness into His marvelous light, are to show forth His glory. The church is the repository of the riches of the grace of Christ . . . ."[41]

With this perspective, when a congregation *(every congregation is seen as consisting of members who are part of the body of Christ, His Church)* is about to be started, it is important that the mother church or the group of individuals, who are seeking to launch the new congregation, be in a healthy state throughout every stage of the process leading up to and during the actual birth of the new congregation.

CONTENTS

With this in mind, it is important to examine the view that a congregation can experience ill-health during its life cycle.

Ill-health and a Congregation's Life Cycle

The period leading up to the launching of a new congregation can be terms "Gestation" which can be a few months prior to the birth of a congregation. In order to move forward healthily with this process, intercessory prayer should prevail throughout the entire process so that there is a healthy delivery of the new congregation.

The Emotional & Spiritual Life Cycle of a Congregation

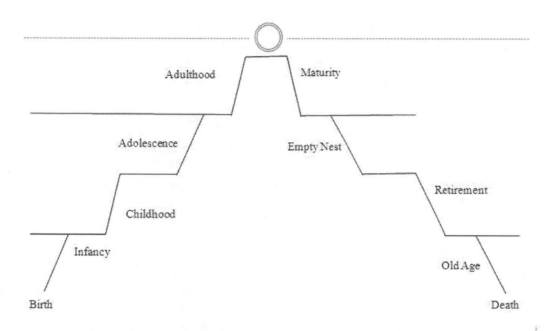

From the diagram above, Phase 1 of a congregation's life consists of birth and infancy, which spans approximately five (5) years. It is true that congregations should move naturally through these stages and experience growth and a healthy development since vision and relationships dominate at stages 2,3,4, and 5. However, those involved in the planting of a new congregation, must remember that healthy mothers generally give birth to healthy babies. Furthermore, the church planters and organisers must ensure that the new congregation is not a product which has emerged from a split or separation, since such circumstances do not give birth to healthy congregations for the short or the long term.

It is interesting to note that relationships become dominant during the redevelopment phase of a congregation's life. However, as the congregations gets older and reaches old age, it tends to lose its

vision and give way to management. It seems then that when vision is placed in the background, a congregation tends to slide towards ill-health, since vision breaths life and spiritual activity.

Some Combinations of a Congregation's Ill-health

A combination of situations indicates that ill-health can set in at any stage of a congregation's life cycle. The following are some of the combinations :

- Healthy congregations can become unhealthy

- Unhealthy congregations remain unhealthy

27

- Vulnerable congregations can become unhealthy

Every congregation which has been launched successfully seeks to create a healthy environment for an opportunity to worship, evangelise, minister and engage in mission. These healthy patterns flow from the fiery passion of these new individuals to fulfil the congregation's strategic spiritual vision.

However, when a congregation lacks a clear long-term vision, or refuses to re-examine the vision, which centres on mission and ministry, it becomes spiritually weak and can easily be affected negatively. Consequently, this lack of a vision can lead to interpersonal problems and therefore, negatively affect the relationships.

As a result, instead of the members becoming involved in the life of the congregation such as fellowship, prayer, evangelistic outreach and bible studies so that they can experience spiritual growth, some of them leave the congregation and at times, leave the church altogether. This unhealthy condition requires the need for the ministry of holistic restoration so that the congregation can re-experience harmony.

Another situation which arises is that unhealthy congregations can remain unhealthy, especially when the leaders are unaware of the health condition. Leaders who do not give attention to a congregation's spirituality, may neglect the opportunity to spot the condition of the congregation's health. However, leaders are advised to " . . . educate your mind to a knowledge of the subjects with which the word of God has amply furnished you, you could build up the cause of God by feeding the flock with food which would be proper and which would give spiritual health and strength as their wants require."[42]

At times, leaders are aware of the ill-health through observation, visitation or prayer. However, they may be unable to or be ill-equipped to address the ill-health. Leaders need to invest some time and energy in unearthing the unhealthy condition that exists. This can be done through much indepth discussions with the eldership team to grasp insight into the situation. Having grasp such understanding, it is important to provide/facilitate a remedy for the illness, either by sourcing knowledgeable individuals who can minister in this area or by conducting sessions in this area.

A third situation is that a congregation can become vulnerable through at least three (3) factors namely:

poor visionary leadership, relational issues and doctrinal issues.

If there is poor visionary leadership or if visionary leadership does not exist, this can contribute to a congregation's ill-health. This can lead to some congregations sauntering on with the run-of-the-mill ministry activities which have no meaningful effect. Leaders are an important element in ensuring the healthy state of a congregation and this begins with developing the vision which is the process that "energizes, informs, shapes, creates a climate, sets a tone, raises the bar, triggers passion, and engenders action."[43] More importantly, leaders must ensure that a vision is created for their congregations since "vision injects purpose and life into an organisation [*and by extension, into a congregation*]."[44]

Relational issues also impact negatively and this is an area which brings about emotional difficulties such an animosity, anger and bitterness. These tend to lead to spiritual problems and can also affect people's physical health. Doctrinal difficulties can also create relational problems, thus causing some members to experience difficulty in assimilating into and become involved in the life of the congregation. It is in these kinds of situations that a congregation needs the ministry of holistic restoration.

Summary

The role which the local congregation plays is very important in relation to nurture and evangelism, two elements which comprise pastoral care. By ignoring the emotional ill-health of a congregation, leaders would find it difficult to provide momentum in the congregation. Since a congregation can become unhealthy at any stage in its life cycle, leaders have the responsibility of monitoring their congregations' health. Furthermore, healthy congregations can become unhealthy through factors such as poor leadership and interpersonal relationships, thus the need for the ministry of holistic restoration which can assist in the implementation of an effective ministry.

6
Phases of Holistic Restoratio

Healing cannot be rushed. It is in light of this view that holistic restoration needs time so that individuals and congregations can experience the impact from the intervention. Ill-health creates imbalance or a disequilibrium in any living organism, be it a person or a congregation. Given that the leaders of a congregation recognise the existence of ill-health, there are four (4) phases through which congregations must go in order to undergo holistic restoration.

CONTENTS

Disequilibrium is the initial phase, consisting of **acknowledgement** and **congregational confession or repentance.** Phase two is the *deliverance* phase which focuses on **forgiveness** and **freedom,** while, the *harmony* phase relates to **reconciliation** and **recovery.** The final phase, *optimal,* deals with **restoration.** Furthermore, the entire process of holistic restoration is grounded on a ministry of intercessory prayer, a spiritual discipline which should prevail throughout the healing process. Having given a brief description of these phases, a more comprehensive discussion will now be given.

Hierarchy of Holistic Restoration Healing

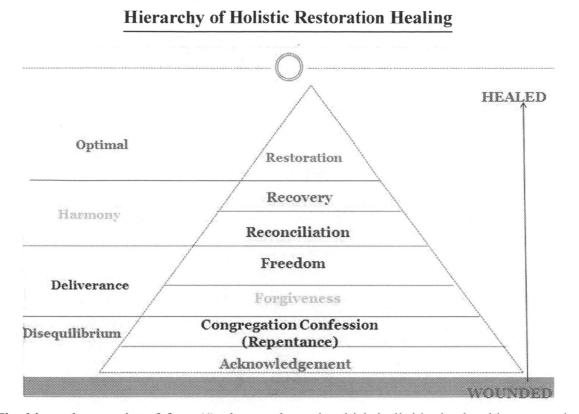

The hierarchy consist of four (4) phases, through which individuals should progressive upwards with the aid of various spiritual disciplines such as intercessory prayer and fasting. There are three (3) parts to this aspect of the ministry: *processes, journeys and steps.* The slidable elements of holistic restoration, which brings about healing in Christian congregations and by extension, in our personal lives, form a hierarchy portrayed graphically as a pyramid (see diagram above).

Processes

The first phase, disequilibrium, consists of two processes: acknowledging and congregational confession all of which impact on us progressively. Additionally, the processes are fundamental, basic and demanding, thus they form the base of the pyramid.

These fundamental processes, which cause spiritual instability or disequilibrium in a congregation, deal with **acknowledging** (admitting and agreeing) that ill-health exists in a congregation/an individual. This attitude is necessary for the bondage and spiritual chains, holding back the congregation, to be broken and for the strongholds in the congregation to be pulled down. Scripture reminds us of the need for this process, when King David, in seeking forgiveness for his sins opened his heart:

> ➢ "For I am conscious of my transgressions and I acknowledge them; my sin is ever before me. Against You, You only, have I sinned and done that which is evil in Your

sight, so that You are justified in Your sentence and faultless in Your judgment" *(Psalm 51:3-4, AMP).*

> I acknowledged my sin to You, and my iniquity I did not hide. I said, I will confess my transgressions to the Lord [continually unfolding the past till all is told]—then You [instantly] forgave me the guilt and iniquity of my sin. Selah [pause, and calmly think of that] *(Psalm 32:5, AMP).*

The prophet, Jeremiah, also substantiated this view.

> Only know, understand, and acknowledge your iniquity and guilt—that you have rebelled and transgressed against the Lord your God and have scattered your favors among strangers under every green tree, and you have not obeyed My voice, says the Lord *(Jeremiah 3:13, AMP).*

The requirement for the next higher process of the hierarchy, that of **congregational confession**, is more demanding and also causes instability and is necessary to move on towards experiencing forgiveness and forgiving others. In this process, the members of the congregation should be helped to go through a time of repentance. More importantly, a congregation that is in spiritual decline, tends to have sin lurking somewhere. Sin has severe consequences and if left un-repented of, can linger long among the people. Sin must be repented of and confessed before a congregation can progress, before revival can take place. Congregational sins which hang over the people's head prevent spiritual growth, and results in people being lethargic, inactive among other unspiritual states and can even lead to backslidden state. Scripture alerts us of the importance of this process:

> "If we confess our sins, he is faithful and just and will forgive us our sins and purify us from all unrighteousness" (**1 John 1:9, NIV**).

> Therefore confess your sins to each other and pray for each other so that you may be healed (**James 5:16, NIV**).

Journeys in Holistic Restorative Healing

There are three (3) journeys in this hierarchy: *forgiveness, freedom and reconciliation.* However, the second class of elements, which consists of two of them: forgiveness and freedom, are more spiritually demanding because they require a higher level of spirituality and they lead to spiritual and emotional deliverance. After

going through the two processes, it is important that members go on these journeys which can be long, painful, difficult and emotional. These journeys, if accepted, move individuals to a deeper spirituality and are more demanding than the previous

processes before them. Each journey has its own set of stages which must be gone through on the way towards restoration and healing.

The journey towards **forgiveness** consists of five stages: 1st)Facing your painful past helps you to overcome it, (2nd) Surrender the Past, (3rd) Leave the Past Behind, (4th) Experiencing Forgiveness, (5th) Move on/Press Forward.

To take the journey towards total **freedom** requires: 1st) Facing the strongholds, (2nd) Surrendering them, (3rd) Pulling down the Strongholds through intercessory prayer and fasting, (4th) Leaving the strongholds Behind, (5th) Injecting/Speaking life/revival, (6th) Unwrapping the layers of your past, (7th) Experiencing the Freedom.

The next set of elements relates to providing harmony in people's life and consists of the last journey, which also has five stages, that being the journey towards **reconciliation**. The stages are (1st) Acknowledge the Problem, (2nd) Accept Consequences, (3rd) Set up an Altar of Sacrifice, (4th) Experience Emotional and Spiritual Revival, (5th) Release from Spiritual Captivity/Reconciliation. Following on from these journeys, we now turn to steps towards holistic restorative healing, the last set of elements.

Steps Towards Holistic Restorative Healing

The final elements of this ministry relates to two steps :(1) **recovery**, and (2) **restoration**. Recovery indicates that one has regained his/her health. This element relates to an experience which occurs after the deliverance phase. Moreover, it is the final stage in the harmony phase, and when experienced, indicates that holistic healing is occurring.

The last of the two steps, restoration, can be seen as a means of self-actualisation. The Greek word used for "restore" means to repair, to fit, frame, or mend. This implies not only that the recipient of restoration was in some sort of disrepair or error, but that there is a pattern by which we must be "framed or fitted". This final element, which is at the top of the hierarchy, defines the *optimal phase* and focuses on 'growth', where individuals are aided in focusing on the 'being' aspect of their lives.

Summary

As we move up the hierarchy, the impact of the elements inter-changes at different levels. They interact among each person, on the divine level and with oneself. These elements pinpoint the importance of each successive element to one's emotional and spiritual health. Moreover, the basic elements are more devastating when they are left un-addressed. In general, we must address the lower elements of the hierarchy before they can move on to deeper spiritual aspects of their lives.

An implication from engaging in this ministry is that when individuals seek to achieve higher elements, they must be aware that the lowers ones impact on the progress of a higher element.

PART C

A Balm in Gilead: An Intervention Strategy

"Is there no balm in Gilead, *Is there* no physician there? Why then is
there no recovery for the health of the daughter of my people?''
(Jer 8:22, NKJV)

7
An Intervention Strategy

CONTENTS

Introduction

The Negro Spiritual entitled *Balm in Gilead* is pertinent for this Section, in that it points to the need for and provides an awareness of an intervention strategy which can aid us in getting rid of the anger, bitterness and hatred which we have nursed because of our wounds. Some individuals who have been wounded develop a deep anger, or animosity towards various individuals and have carried this negative emotion for years. However, such individuals can be assured that "There is a Balm in Gilead to make the wounded whole; There is a balm in Gilead to heal the sin-sick soul."

As Jeremiah mourned for the Israelites, he made a pertinent remark and sought to stir us as seen in Jeremiah 8:21-22:

> For the hurt of the daughter of my people I am hurt.
> I am mourning;
> Astonishment has taken hold of me.
> *Is there* no balm in Gilead,
> *Is there* no physician there?
> Why then is there no recovery
> For the health of the daughter of my people?

In fact, this is a real question and a burning issue: *Is there* no balm in Gilead, *Is there* no physician there? with which many individuals have been and are struggling with even today.

Part **C: A Balm in Gilead—An Intervention Strategy** provides four sections which are beneficial in aiding you in experiencing healing for your wounds. *A Journey Towards*

Forgiveness highlights the need to reach a stage in our lives where we can extend and receive forgiveness through which we begin to experience healing. Having been forgiven, this helps us to experience freedom so that we can rid ourselves of the anger that we may have developed. This is a crucial step and as a result leads us to the place where we need to engage in reconciliation so that we can experience holistic healing.

A Journey Towards Forgiveness

Aim: To help individuals understand how our painful past can affect our spiritual journey, and therefore, encourage individuals to be willing to move ahead.

Philippians 3:7-14 provides an essential principle: when we hold onto our painful past experiences and memories, we lose opportunities for spiritual and emotional progress. However, the previous verses, (vv **3-6**) provide brief and insightful details about the Apostle Paul's background. This biblical character shared insights about his past behaviour, thoughts and attitude. We get a glimpse of his status is society and his various achievements. But why did he decide to stir up his past life. He realised that in order to move forward, he must go backward. With this in mind, let us examine this journey towards forgiveness.

Stage 1: Facing Your Painful Past Helps You Overcome It.

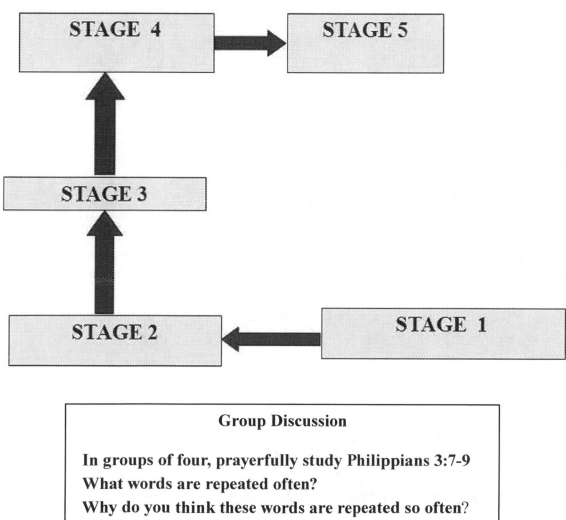

```
STAGE 4  ──►  STAGE 5

  ▲

STAGE 3

  ▲

STAGE 2  ◄──  STAGE 1
```

Group Discussion

In groups of four, prayerfully study Philippians 3:7-9
What words are repeated often?
Why do you think these words are repeated so often?

In verses **7-14**, Paul is focusing on someone else. He described his previous lifestyle in order to confront and face the things that hindered him from tapping into the saving grace of Christ. There are deep-seated issues in our lives that we have never dealt with and they are hindering our spirituality, hindering our relationship with Christ. We need to face them head on. Just like Paul, we also need to face our painful memories and our adverse experiences. Sometimes the things that happen, the things we do and say are ugly, painful, devastating and shameful. Our behaviours and attitudes are disturbing. But we need to look at them and address them.

Stage 2: The solution for a painful past is to surrender it.

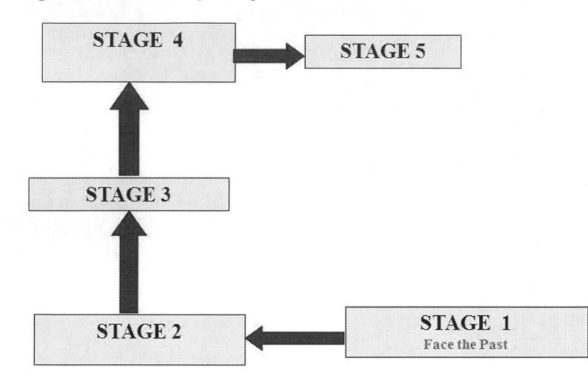

Our past hurts and deeds may be painful, but we need to engage in the surrendering process. Psychologically, when our minds are filled with un-surrendered painful memories, it makes it difficult for us to experience happiness. Consequently, we carry thoughts of revenge in our minds, we become angry, bitter and anxious. God cares about our spiritual progress and that's why he reminds us to:

[18] **"Forget the former things;**
do not dwell on the past.

[19] **See, I am doing a new thing!**
Now it springs up; do you not perceive it?
I am making a way in the desert
and streams in the wasteland (Isa 43:18-19, NIV)

The God of Heaven wants to bring about spiritual renewal, tear away our past hurtful issues and help us to progress with our spiritual lives. Additionally, He wants (1) to bring relief and deliverance, and (2) for us to reach a place where we can connect with Him and experience spiritual progress.

In order for us to turn away from our painful past, the hurts and injustice done to us requires boldness, and it calls for a willingness to do what is right even if we are criticised. It calls for spiritual strength to face the challenges. We can **no longer hold onto to our painful past**. We are encouraged to surrender them to Jesus. At this stage, we need to spend time in prayer and be honest with God about what has happened to us, how we feel, and what was done to us. Here is where we need to forgive others, forgive ourselves, and ask for forgiveness.

It is important to note that "the condition of the mind affects the health to a far greater degree than many realise. Grief, anxiety, discontent, remorse, guilt, distrust all tend to break down the life forces and to invite decay and death."[45]

Stage 3: Leave the Past Behind

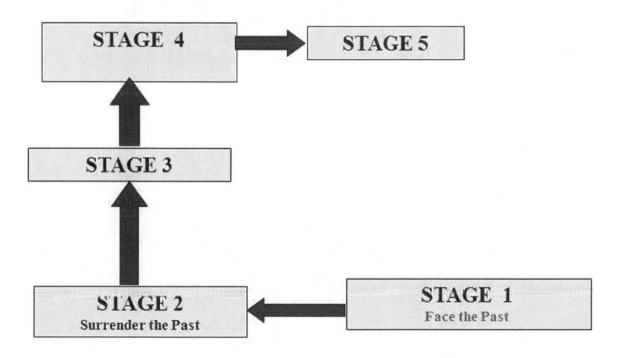

According to Phil 4:13, in order for us to move forward in our spiritual journey, we must leave the past behind, by turning away from it. One way of doing this could be by writing out the issues on a sheet of paper and lay them at your 'altar' and pray about them. Ask God to clear your thoughts and mind of the issue or event. Afterwards, shred/burn the paper(s) as a sign of getting rid of the issues. The Evil One wants to keep you living in the past. He fills our mind with those negative feelings and events and we keep focusing on them. Such experiences dwell in the subconscious section of our mind.

There are two main sections of the mind: the conscious and the subconscious sections . Most of our behaviours, anger disturbing thoughts, jealousy and negative attitudes are hidden in the subconscious (unconscious) section of the mind. These things affect our self esteem, our behaviour to each other and our view of our life and of other people.

Figure 1: Psychological Sections of the Mind

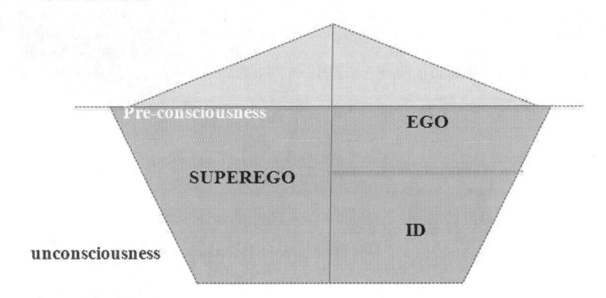

It takes the power of the Holy Spirit to turn around the mind, to clear the subconscious (unconscious) mind and to give it a new focus.

Group Discussion

Choose ONE Text: Rom 6:6; Rom 8:35-37;2 Cor. 5:17 and reflect on it
What changes can we experience in our lives?
How does the Word of God assist us with our past hurtful situations?

Stage 4: Experience Forgiveness and Healing

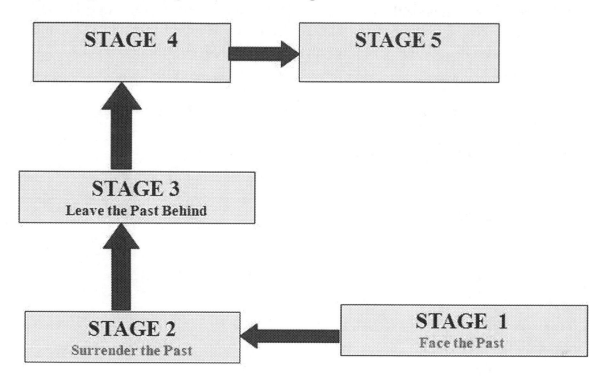

Facing our hurts, painful memories and the disappointments, surrendering them and leaving them behind allows healing to take place. God has promised that "He heals the broken hearted and binds up their wounds" (Psalm 147:3). King David acknowledged his sins as seen in Ps 51. Jacob was forgiven by God, and there was healing (Gen 33). Joseph forgave his brothers and experienced healing (Gen 45, 50). Peter experienced forgiveness and was healed (Lk 22.54, 23:34). It's the first step towards experiencing healing **for the mind, for the spirit and even healing for the body.** When we face those painful memories such as injustice, bitterness, hatred for someone, hurts and regrets, we become emotionally strong and spiritually free, even though we cry bitterly.

Reaching this stage of the journey helps us to see where we are in Christ. As we take this journey, we come one step closer to experiencing inner peace, We too can bring peace to a trouble soul or a perplexed individual.

It is important to note that forgiveness improves our mental and physical well being. It reduces stress and improves blood pressure and heart rate. When we go through this stage, we need to be aware that . . .

> **. . . forgiveness starts from on the inside of us. It helps you the forgiver FISRT, It gives you peace of mind. We hold the keys to forgiveness. It is our choice, to leave our home, church, your community in turmoil or extend forgiveness, by taking this journey.**

43

Psychologically, when we forgive others, we experience less anxiety, and stress. There is a decreased in our negative thoughts, less grief, less anger, our relationships with others improve and we have a better perspective on life and we see God for whom he really is. When we deal with the anger that is in us, then we can experience peace and calm between others and ourselves.

Stage 5: Seeing the Spiritual Prize Motivates us to Move on/Press Forward

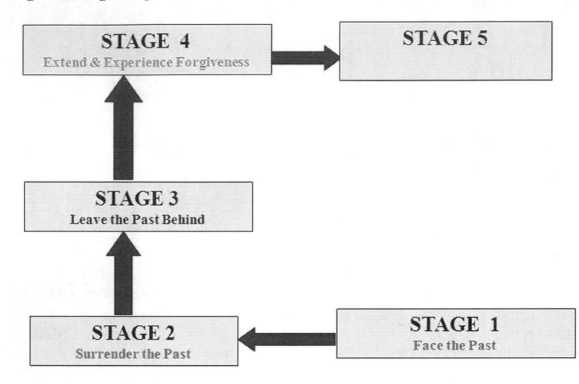

It is at this point that we need to reach forward for what is ahead. That is why verse 14 is important here: "I press on towards the goal to win the prize for which God has called me heavenwards in Christ Jesus." God expects us to make the effort to move on, strive forward and press on. The importance of striving is stressed because the idea is repeated often in **vv12, 13, 14.**

We must strive as though our salvation depends on us and we must pray earnestly as though our salvation depends on God. Scripture reminds us that we "are a chosen race, a royal priesthood, a holy nation, God's own people, in order that you may proclaim the mighty acts of him who called you out of darkness into his marvelous light" (1 Pet 2:9, NRSV).

Our desire should be to know Christ and experience the power that raised Him from the dead. This helps us to take what Christ has achieved for us: Salvation, spiritual victory, redemption and reconciliation to God. It is important to strive forward so that we can focus on our spiritual inheritance because we are heirs of God and joint heirs with Jesus. This journey which we have just embarked on awakens us to the need to go backwards in order to go forward. By doing this, we are in a better position to experience total freedom.

A Journey Towards Total Freedom

Aim: To help individuals become aware of the impact of emotional and spiritual strongholds on their Christian life and identify ways to experience freedom.

Some twenty (20) years after Joseph is sold as a slave, dispatched and gotten rid of, and wiped off the scene by his brothers, they now fall into his hands. God is so all-knowing that he allows events to occur in our lives to wake us up. A severe famine takes place and 10 brothers are facing their innocent brother. With the passing of time, change of appearance, new clothes and possibly a new hairstyle, **Genesis 42:8** reminds us that "although Joseph recognized his brothers, they didn't recognize him." Such a revelation created a new world. How interesting it is when our life is on the line, and when we are threatened with life and death. This seems to be time when individuals become honest and are willing to make any promise, no matter how unrealistic. The brothers' lives are on the line and now they seek to be honest. How Ironic! The same boys that almost killed the dreamer; the same boys that hatched a plan and deceived the deceiving Jacob, their father, are now honest in **v 13!**

This scene is packed with drama, action, and a lot of events are taking place: the brothers were spoken to roughly, called spies, and then thrown into prison for three days. They are also threatened and finally, guilt hung over their heads almost permanently. As Joseph weeps, we can ask: Are they tears of joy, sorrow, repentance, forgiveness, pity or compassion? What was going through Joseph's mind: revenge, get even, u made me waste many precious years of my life in prison . . . its payback time, leave them to starve?

These ten (10) guilty brothers are not the ones in trouble here. These are not the ones who need releasing, or who need to be set free. It is Joseph, the innocent brother. He seems trapped in a battle between getting revenge and showing a compassionate heart. So how do we break such a yoke, chain, or stronghold in our lives? How do you get freedom from such emotional captivity?

In examining Genesis 43:29-31, we would agree that often times we are unable from an emotional and psychological perspective, to face the person that wronged us. But to move on, to be freed or to be rescued, we need to face that issue/person/situation.

Stage 1: Face the situation.

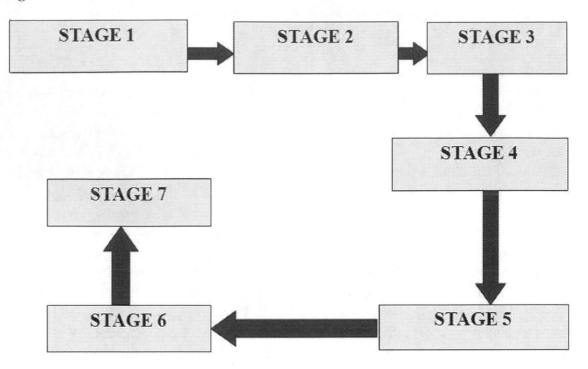

Stage 2: Surrender the Situation

Second, we need to surrender that situation/give it over to Christ in prayer.

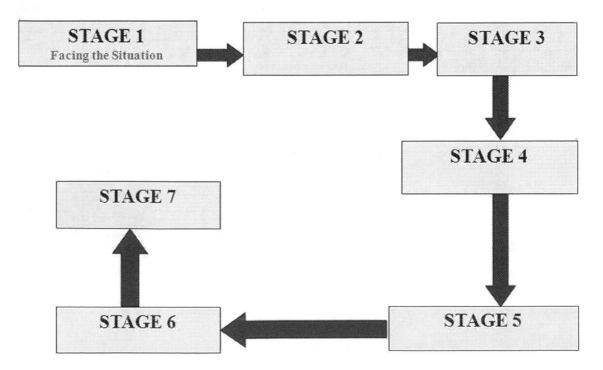

J W van Deventer's song *All to Jesus I surrender,* seems appropriate because for too long, individuals have been holding on to those situations that are only pulling them down and destroying them. It is noted that " . . . all angels have been near to Christ's faithful followers. The vast confederacy of evil is arrayed against all who would overcome; but Christ would have us look to the things which are not seen, to the armies of heaven encamped about all who love God, to deliver them. From what dangers, seen and unseen, we have been preserved through the interposition of the angels, we shall never know, until in the light of eternity we see the providences of God. Then we shall know that the whole family of heaven was interested in the family here below, and that messengers from the throne of God attended our steps from day to day."[46] Moreover, surrendering our situations to God involves writing out the issues on paper as much as we can. In doing this, you begin to engage in writing therapy which helps you to flush your system of the issue. Additionally, it is important to engage in the activity on **Pages 19-20** of this Resource Guide. Progressing into the next stage, we need Christ to break the chains/strongholds in our life.

Stage 3: Pull Down/Break the Strongholds Through Prayer and Fasting

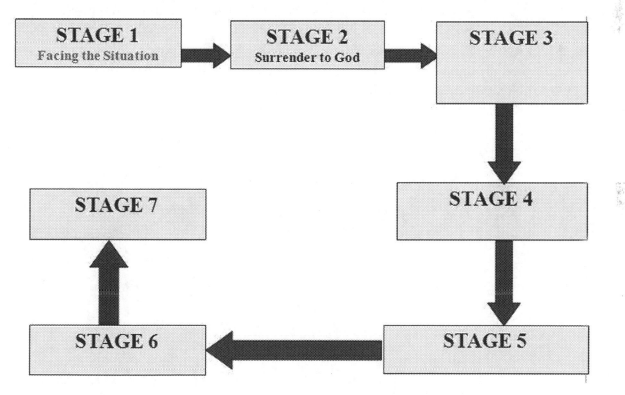

Christ reminds us in Luke 4:18 of his mission to this earth:

"The Spirit of the Lord is on me,
because he has anointed me
to proclaim good news to the poor.
He has sent me to proclaim freedom for the prisoners
and recovery of sight for the blind,
to set the oppressed free" (NIV).

In fact, the New King James Version renders the clause 'proclaim freedom for the captives' as 'proclaims liberty to the captives'. The New International Version uses the clause' to proclaim freedom for the prisoners' and the Amplified Bible renders it as 'announce release to the captives'. Second Corinthians 10:4-6 helps us to understand the need for breaking strongholds in our lives. In particular, verse 4 puts this issue in perspective: "For the weapons of our warfare are not carnal, but mighty through God to the pulling down of strong holds." The fact that we are engaged in a spiritual battle and in a conflict, indicates that we are fighting adversity, calamity, distress, and carnal behaviour among others. The intense battle is played out in the spiritual realm, with Christ gaining the victory for us at Calvary Cross. Such barriers need drastic measures which can come through intercessory prayer, fasting, pleading the blood of Christ, inviting Christ into your live, applying the Word of God to our situation and by being anointed. Having broken the strongholds, we need to leave the issues at the altar.

Stage 4:Leave Strongholds at the Altar

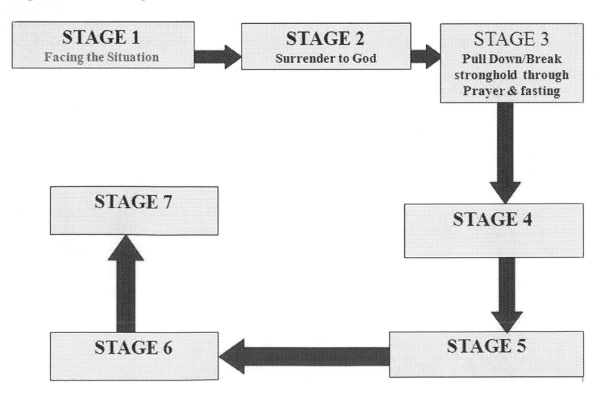

In order to experience the freedom that Christ has achieved for us at Calvary's Cross, it is important that we bring the issue on the sheet of paper to Christ through prayer at your altar of sacrifice. As we plead to God in intercessory prayer, it is also acceptable and spiritually powerful to burn that list of issues, vowing not to return to it or let it into your life again. Having reached this stage, we need to speak life into our new situation.

Stage 5: Speak Life

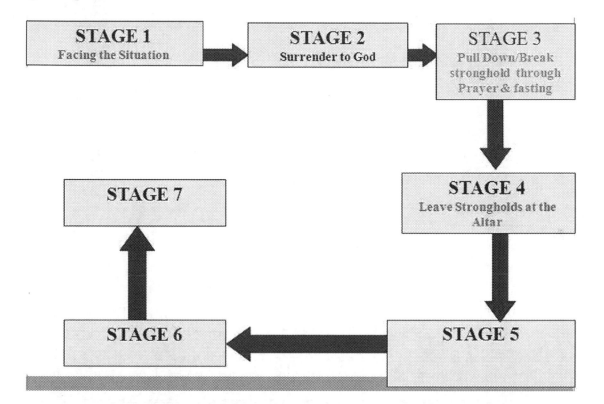

At this stage, you need a spiritual revival, a resurrection and a renewal of life. It would be beneficial at this time to focus on **Page 24** of this Resource Guide. Additionally, by focusing on the Scriptures, we can experience the living power of God from studying and reading His Word. Jesus spoke life to Lazarus, by initially commanding the people to remove the blockages and then speaking to Lazarus directly (Jn 11:38,44). By studying, memorising, and reading aloud the Word of God, we need to allow it to speak to us about the different issues such as suicidal thoughts (Isaiah 26:3) or calamity (Psalm 34:19)

Following on from this is the need to unwrap the layers of our painful past.

Stage 6: Unwrap the Layers of Our Past

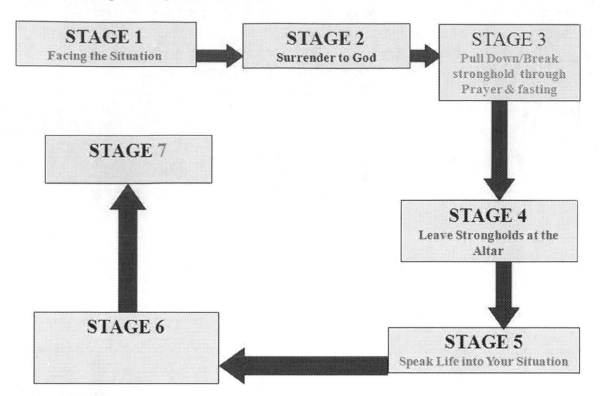

After Jesus spoke life into Lazarus by resurrecting him, there was still the need for him to be released from the grave-clothes, the symbols of death (Jn 11:44). However, some situations may need to be unwrapped tenderly, by addressing one aspect (layer) at a time, especially when the situation is very sensitive. Unwrapping the layers of our painful past signals a need for a new lifestyle and new thoughts, thereby experiencing a transformation.

Personal Prayer

Prayerfully reflect on 2 Corinthians 5:17. Spend some time praying for yourself using this text.

On turning away from the old lifestyle and inviting Jesus into our lives, we can be assured that there is no condemnation in our hearts (Rom 8:1). This is important since Christ came into the world so that we can have life in abundance (Jn 10:10). When we address and throw off our painful past life, this leads to the time of freedom.

Stage 7: Step into & Experience Freedom

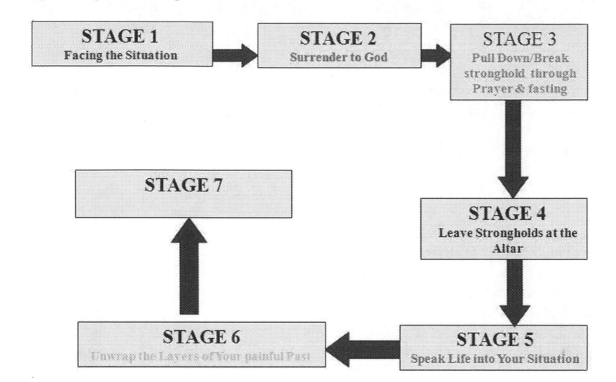

Jesus, having raised Lazarus from the dead and requested that his grave-clothes be taken off, assured the new living being of his freedom. Lazarus was set free and similarly Christ, by coming into our lives, aids us in experiencing freedom. Importantly, un-Christian behaviours and attitudes towards others have negative consequences on us and if they are not surrendered to Christ, can hinder our spiritual progress.

Escaping Your Pit Without Being Angry

AIM: To assist individuals in identifying processes which can contribute to the development of positive emotional health and spiritual maturity.

"Be angry, and do not sin, do not let the sun go down on your wrath," (Eph 4:26, NKJV), yet many of us become angry as a result of suffering from various situations. It's a human response to difficult situations. But how can we experience victory without living with anger, bitterness and hatred? This presentation seeks to address this question.

Level 1: Be Aware of Divine Presence

As Christians, when we go through trials and difficulties, it is essential that we involve the Lord into the situation and have faith that God is with us as we see with Joseph, the biblical character. Inspite of the fact that Joseph was in prison, Scripture reminds us that "his master saw that the Lord was with him and that the Lord made all he did to prosper in his hand" (Gen 39:3,NKJV).

Fill in the empty box

Level 1

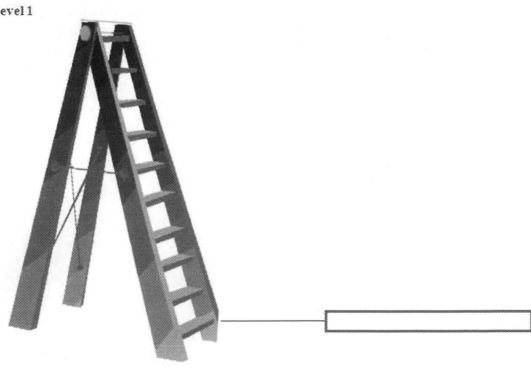

Genesis 39:21 also reminds us of God's presence with Joseph which accounted for all of his success in prison and in Potiphar's house and his promotion to a level of authority.

Level 2: Honour God

Secondly, in order to escape out emotional or spiritual pit, we must honour Yahweh, who directs our paths. As we face more dilemmas similar to Joseph, we must be prepared to resist the enemy, as Joseph did when he was tempted by Potiphar's wife (Gen 39:9-14)

Fill in the empty box

Level 2

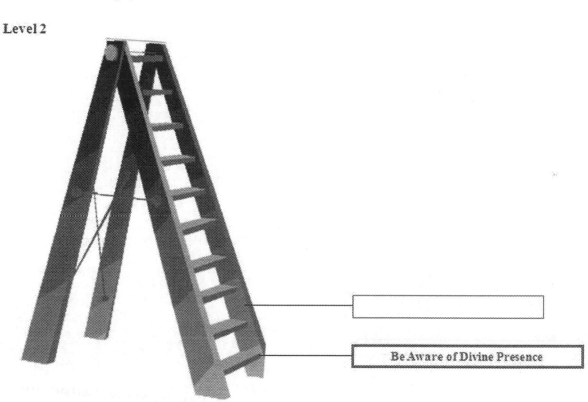

Be Aware of Divine Presence

More importantly, it is important to share our faith in God wisely, thereby identifying with God's people as Joseph did: "For indeed I was stolen away from the land of the Hebrews; and also I have done nothing here that they should put me into the dungeon." (Gen 40:15, NKJV). When we anchor our spiritual identity, this helps us to reframe our struggles and be aware that we cannot rely on human being since they can fail us (Gen 40:23; Jer 17:5-8)

Group Study

Prayer Study Gen 41: 16-45

• In what ways was Joseph honouring God ?

Level 3:Living in God's Directive Will

Christians use a very powerful spiritual weapon, that of intercessory prayer, whereby divine intervention provides greater effect. By engaging in intercessory prayer, this helps us to know God's will for our lives. Although there are two wills: directive (submissive) and permissive, God desires that we be in his directive will, where we allow Him to guide and direct our lives and plans.

Fill in the empty box

Level 3

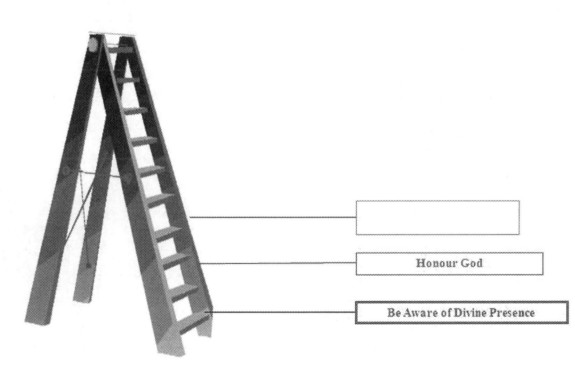

Honour God

Be Aware of Divine Presence

As God's children, it is the submissive or directive will for our lives that we should seek to know, whereby we can be obedient to Him and live a life of inner peace. It is not an opportunity to dictate to God or to get Him to do what we want, but to discover what is God's will for our individual life and/or the congregation.

Christians use a very powerful spiritual weapon, that of intercessory prayer, whereby divine intervention is given greater effect.

Level 4: Be An Agent for God

The Apostle Paul reminds us that ". . . we are ambassadors for Christ, as though God were pleading through us: we implore *you* on Christ's behalf, be reconciled to God" (2 Cor. 5.20). Ambassadors speak for their countries and leaders, to get their countries' viewpoint across to the host country and by extension, to the world.

Fill in the empty box

Level 4

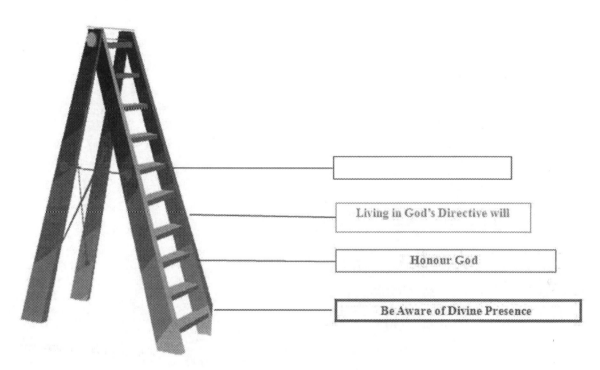

Genesis 40:8-23 indicates that Joseph was an agent for God and made a great impact on his surroundings, to the point that he began rising from his pit. Joseph, similar to Paul, focused on his divine-directed status, that of ambassador, as opposed to his imposed status, that of prisoner. This helps us to keep our faith in the Almighty One and progress further as we endeavour to rise out of the pit.

Level 5:Experiencing Divine Elevation

An important process in escaping from our pit is rising near the top of the pit. However, many people will see the Hand of God on your life and will acknowledge this fact as was with Joseph (Gen 41:27-45). Pharaoh confirmed that God was with Joseph and through this, God used the heathen to bless Joseph.

Fill in the empty box

Level 5

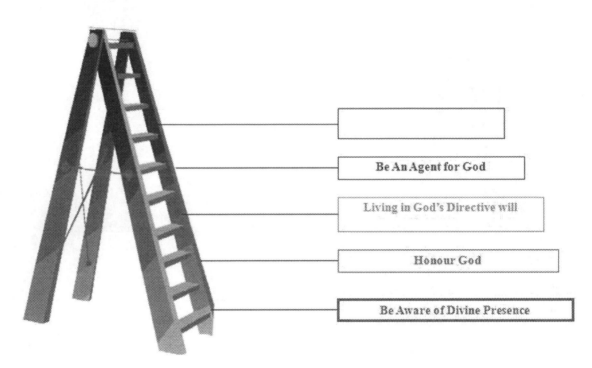

Level 6:Humility: One Step from Victory

As we get closer to the top of our pit, it is important that we remain humble in the eyes of God and our fellowmen. The hunger for retaliation tends to overpower us, and causes us to dishonour God and allows the enemy to defeat us. Joseph was one step away from reaching the top of his pit. It is therefore important for us to use tact and be wise as we get closer to our victory.

Fill in the empty box

Level 6

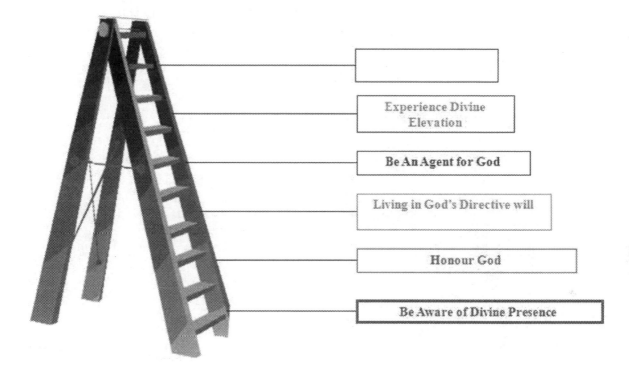

Experience Divine Elevation

Be An Agent for God

Living in God's Directive will

Honour God

Be Aware of Divine Presence

DISCUSSION

- After reading Gen 41:14-36, share your thoughts on how Joseph could have reacted, based on all the difficulties that he had experienced.

Level 7:Keeping the Heart for God

Reaching the top of our pit is similar to experiencing healing for our wounds. Based on this view, when we are healed we carry the scars to show what we have been through along the way. However, the pain goes away and the impact of the wound disappears. Nevertheless, we tend to remember the difficulties when something or someone triggers the event.

Fill in the empty box

Level 7

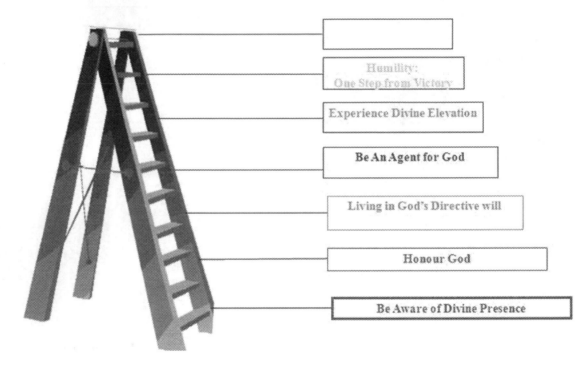

Joseph had a similar experience and to demonstrate that he was healed, he named his first-born son, Manasseh, meaning forgetful (Gen 41:51). His heart was dedicated to and set aside for God, who had allowed him to be in Egypt for a purpose. Consequently, he became a blessing to many including his own siblings. Similarly, when we rise to the top of our pit, and have experienced a transformation, it is essential that, through the power of the Holy Spirit, we produce positive thoughts, engage in desirable behaviours and display Christ-like attitudes that can benefit other individuals.

A Journey Towards Reconciliation

The entire book of 2nd Samuel deals with battles; From Israel and Judah fighting each other to Joab killing Abner. Absalom attacks and kills his brother Ammon. David is on the run from his own son, Absalom. Bloodshed is common in this book, with Absalom's death. David is featured prominently in this book, as a mighty warrior, brave, courageous and ruthless, no–nonsense King. Throughout the episodes, we see God leading, and protecting David, yet he focused on his human army, thus deciding to count the soldiers. Such a sin displeased God, leading to it hanging over the Israelites' head.

The Israeli nation is unable to move forward because both the King and the leaders are pre–occupied with the King's sinful deed. **How do we rebuild such broken bridges? How do we reconcile with those who have injured/hurt and caused us pain? How do we engage in reconciliation when we are the one who has caused the pain?**

In understanding **congregation reconciliation,** let's examine five (5) stages in the process. On examining 2 Sam **24:10-14,** we see that leaders play a crucial role in the spiritual development of a congregation. Pastoral leaders have great influence (2 Sam 24.4), thus they are ultimately responsible to God for His people in this process.

Stage 1: Acknowledge the Problem

Fill in the empty box

RE-BUILDING BROKEN BRIDGES

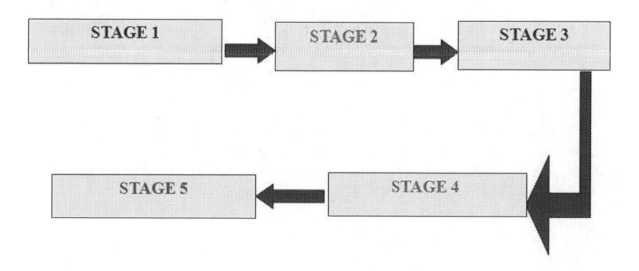

In reflecting on verses 10 and 17, we notice that David was honest, having reached the point where his heart condemned him. Condemnation brings guilt and shame. *A Congregation that is preparing for battle must search itself through prayer.* Leaders have the awesome task of getting this process started with critical soul-searching questions: Where it the congregation spiritually? What's happening ? Is the congregation moving forward, backward or stagnant, or is it on a plateau? Answers to such questions can only come when leaders spent time searching prayerfully.

Stage 2: Accept Consequences

A congregation/individual that is in spiritual decline no doubt has sin lurking somewhere. Sin has severe consequences. It is ugly and if left un-repented of, can linger long among the people.

Fill in the empty box

RE-BUILDING BROKEN BRIDGES

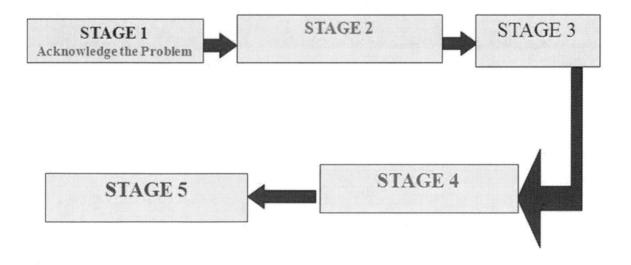

With this in mind, sin has consequences and must be repented of and confessed before a congregation can progress, and before revival can take place. Congregational/ personal sin hanging over the our head prevents spiritual growth or baptism. People are lethargic, inactive and even backsliding. There is a need for *congregational confession to God.*

GROUP SESSION:

Choose one of these text—Dan 9:3-19; Neh 1:5-11:
How intentional were these prophets about engaging in confession and repentance?

Focusing on David's situation, in verses **11 to 14, we notice that he took the divine punishment.** When God chastens, it brings pain at first. His punishment comes because of love as seen in Heb 12:6-7. Indeed, un-confessed sinful behaviours are punished severely but with grace. Furthermore, we are reminded that He *[David]* felt that God knew the struggle and anguish of the soul. When one is enabled to catch a glimpse of the character of God, he sees not in Him the heartless, vindictive spirit manifested by human agents; he sees that affliction and trial are God's appointed means of disciplining His children, and teaching them His way, that they may lay hold of His grace.[47]

We see the God of Heaven giving David three (3) choices: plague, famine, or war. However, David preferred to go through divine punishment, one that echoes the sentiments in Rom 5:20, knowing that the tender mercies of man are cruel. That is the reason David preferred to fall into the Hand of God. Thus, we see David pleading for God's mercies in **verse 17.** Since leaders have ultimate responsibility, they must accept the blame for a congregation's decline. With that being the case we move to the next stage in the process.

Stage 3:Set up the altar of sacrifice

Fill in the empty box

RE-BUILDING BROKEN BRIDGES

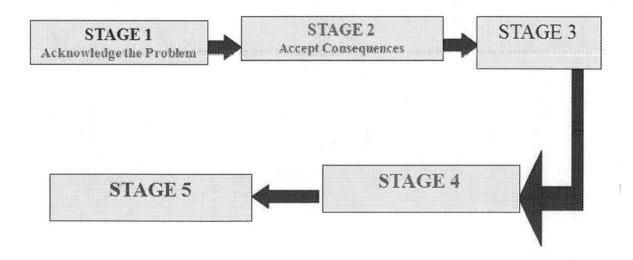

Notice **the divine instructions** in verse 18. It's at our altar that we come to God while sacrificing time and even meals at times. The altar is for slaying sacrifices. Worshipping God has a human cost in that it requires us to make sacrifices (Rom 12:1-2). It's here that we slay our hearts and bring our sacrifice of pleasure, time and money to God. When God restores us, we can show our gratitude with a thank-you offering among other ways. God extends his grace to us, hence sin must be addressed knowing His requirements are pinpointed in **Psalm 66:18.** Note that we must always find our altars, know where it is and never let the fire go out. Through prayer, it is kept burning. Whatever we bring to God must cost us something in time, sweat, prayer and effort. Emerging out of the prayer session, comes revival and reformation of heart and thoughts. It's our responsibility to seek for a revival and be willing intentionally to change or be transformed. Additionally, the congregation must be led into a time of re-commitment and re-consecration.

Stage 4: Experience Emotional and Spiritual Healing

Note that if there is no forgiveness, healing cannot take place. As seen in **verse 25,** God responded to David's intercessory prayer for the people. Not only was prayer offered, but a sacrifice was also made. A sincere heart will repent before the Holy God and seek healing from wrong-doing.

Fill in the empty box

RE-BUILDING BROKEN BRIDGES

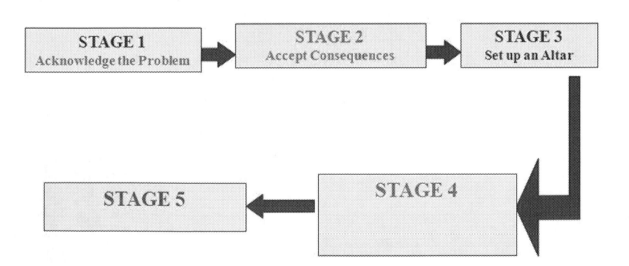

STAGE 1
Acknowledge the Problem

STAGE 2
Accept Consequences

STAGE 3
Set up an Altar

STAGE 5

STAGE 4

Stage 5: Release from Spiritual/Emotional Captivity.

It's here that the punishment is lifted (v 25). Through this Israel was reconciled to God and so can we knowing that Christ also came to build the broken bridge between us and God as seen in **2 Cor 5:18-20. This helps with spiritual deliverance and release from congregational sin.** Moreover, with reconciliation taking place, the congregation can proceed and accomplish the mission that God has set for it.

Fill in the empty box

RE-BUILDING BROKEN BRIDGES

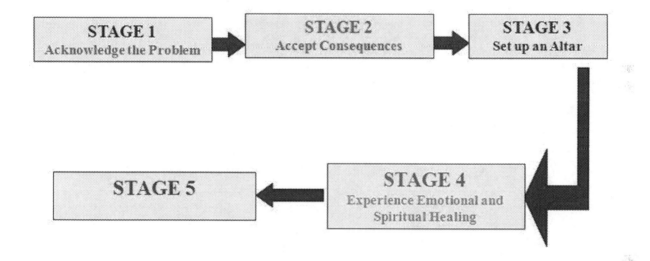

As we go on this journey, may we be willing to endure the difficulties and the uneasiness that it may cause. It is God's desire that we prosper, and experience good health as our soul prospers.

PART D

The Impact of the Ministry of Holistic Restoration

"I *am* the Lord, and *there is* no other; I form the light and create darkness, I make peace and create calamity; I, the Lord, do all these *things*" (Isa 45:6-7, NKJV)

Introduction

Over the years, contemporary Christian church leaders have grappled with problems of varying nature. Leaders have been confronted with problems from doctrinal issues to interpersonal conflicts, from financial unfaithfulness to desecration of the place of worship and from spiritual lethargy to emotional ill-health. Such issues gnaw at the spiritual core of every Christian congregation and severely impacts on the major biblical mandate, that of sharing

CONTENTS

the Gospel of Christ, as is clearly commanded: " Then Jesus came to them and said, 'All authority in heaven and on earth has been given to me. [19] Therefore go and make disciples of all nations, baptising them in the name of the Father and of the Son and of the Holy Spirit, [20] and teaching them to obey everything I have commanded you. And surely I am with you always, to the very end of the age" (Mt 28:18-20, NIV).

Some of the leaders have seen their problems resolved, while others have not experienced any success. And so, conscientious Christian leaders are faced with the searching question: How can we resolve the various problems which exist in the congregation? Nevertheless, another pointed question which could be asked is : Why is it that some church leaders are able to identify and address specific issues in a congregations and others are not?

In an attempt to assist such leaders, this section focuses primarily on emotional and spiritual ill-health of different Christian congregations. The heart of this section is the three (3) cases from ministry in and with various congregations where I have employed a particular strategy. It is important to note that the resources below are not the be all and end all, but have been included to provide encouragement, and to demonstrate how growth and excellence can be accomplish as we engage in practical theology.

The ministry of holistic restoration is not mainly theoretical. It consists of a number of elements such as implementing spiritual disciplines such as intercessory prayer and fasting. Additionally, it involves assessments, observations and the application of spiritual approaches and strategies to various situations. In order to demonstrate this practice, the following cases have been presented below:

- Blackwell Family Church
- Rochester Church
- Well's Praise Centre

Case A: Blackwell Church

Background

Blackwell Church is located in a town of about 65 000 people, with the town situated on the inside of its rural geographical region. There were about forty (40) members during the time we worshipped at this congregation, however the number has reached some 80 +. Additionally, the membership consisted of individuals mainly

from the African continent, and some from the Caribbean, Asia and Eastern Europe. Since the pre-1980s, the members have been worshipping in about three or four locations prior to acquiring their own church building. About a quarter of the membership consists of the youth (14-35 years), while the average age of the membership is 42 years old. This rural congregation is built around families, with there being six (6) major families that make up half of the membership. I also discovered that we had had twelve (12) pastors in this congregation in ten (10) years, thus highlighting a very short pastoral tenure.

> **As I became involved in the life of Blackwell Church, I observed that there was a lack of momentum, low motivation, low spirituality, unavailability of many members for worship services and many of the other services of the church.**

Additionally, there were no ministry plans in place. As a result of this, we began focusing on the spirituality of the members by praying weekly and fasting monthly. Additionally, after discussing with the Church Board the need for a weekly daytime prayer service, a number of members regularly attended the daytime prayer service, apart from the mid-week prayer meeting.

During the subsequent months, as I ministered to the congregation, observed situations and visited members, severe financial unfaithfulness among some members and a mammoth breach of stewardship principles in the treasury emerged. A few members had borrowed money from other members and had refused to repay, and even after many months when the lenders had requested their money, the recipients still refused to repay. Actually, the financial unfaithfulness emerged a month prior to the beginning of the evangelistic campaign for this congregation. This threw us into a state of difficulty and spiritual chaos. Furthermore, the relationship between many church members had deteriorated severely to the point that there were conflicts, harsh

tension, and poor interpersonal relationship. As a result, this un-Christlike behaviour led to emotional and spiritual ill-health in the congregation, and therefore hindered the congregation from progressing spiritually.

During the course of the next few months, an act of discipline occurred. Of the two methods of discipline for our denominational church, the lesser form was agreed to and administered, even though some members wanted to 'draw blood' to obtain their 'pound of flesh'. This conflict, poor interpersonal relationship and the transgression hung over this congregation and it became difficult to move forward.

I recognised that forgiveness or lack of it was at the heart of the problem in this congregation and immediately we searched for an individual who specialises in family therapy to assist us in addressing the problem. Although I was trained in psychology and theology, I felt inadequate to address this serious issue. Nevertheless, we sourced an international family therapist and shared the general issue with her.

Intervention & Strategy

Having discussed the situation in the congregation with the resource person, this therapist agreed to conduct four sessions over a weekend, focusing on various aspects of family issues and the impact these issues have on us. Some of the topics

were: the negative impact of forgiveness on emotional health and trans-generational curses. The final session was a time for questions and answers, when individuals submitted their questions prior to the session so that they could be perused and preparation could be made.

Additionally, an anointing service took place at the end of the mid-day service, during which time many individuals were anointed and prayer for according to their

issues. Moreover, during this special session, the resource person encouraged the entire congregation to spend time in prayer for each other while many were being ministered to on that day.

Impact of the Ministry

The effectiveness of these therapeutic sessions cannot be over-stated. I believe we used the appropriate approach to address the issue. In fact, news about this programme spread throughout the region and had attracted much discussion, especially in relation to the public anointing and the topic on trans-generational curses.

It assisted the members in the congregation to see the need to offer forgiveness and as time progressed, I sensed a change in the atmosphere in the congregation and in the relationships among the members. Healing had begun, even though it took about one year to resolve the issues fully.

However, the members became very active, and the weekly attendance had double its original membership, and more on many occasions. Two evangelistic campaigns were done that year and about eight (8) special days were held per quarter.

The following year, two more evangelistic campaigns were conducted and this congregation hosted a major evangelistic training programme for all the churches in its geographical region.

On reflection, there were no baptisms in the congregation that year of the intervention, even though there was momentum in the congregation and motivation among the members. Moreover, I believed that further specific follow-up should have been carried out through specific sermons and afternoon presentations on related topics. However, owing to my lack of experience in this area, this was not done, even though the daytime prayer services continued. Nevertheless, during our time in this congregation, eighteen (18) individuals were baptised.

Conclusion

Contemporary Christian leaders often grapple with how to resolve the many issues in their congregations. However, although no specific problem is unique, every congregation has a variety of problems that can impact negatively on its mission, if they are left unresolved. The specific issue in this case dealt with unfaithfulness, with the lack of forgiveness emerging as a symptom. Based on this case, I have discovered that healing takes time and cannot be rushed. Moreover, it is important to integrate areas of psychotherapy, counselling, spiritual disciplines (fasting, prayer, etc) and evangelistic outreach in order to bring about the desired healing.

Case B: Rochester Church

Background

Rochester Community Church is located in a town of about 70 000 people, with the town situated on the inside of its rural geographical region. There were about forty (40) members during the time we worshipped at this congregation, a number which has not changed. Additionally, the majority of members are from

Western Europe. The members have been worshipping in their present building since the 1940s. About a quarter of the membership is elderly (65 years +), while the average age of the membership is 50 years old. This rural congregation is built around families, with there being three (3) major families that make up approximately half of the membership.

In the early months we spent worshipping at this congregation, we discovered that no plans had been put in place. We were into the fourth month and there were still no plans. After the pastoral leaders met and shared the direction for the congregation, plans were brought to the Church Board. The meeting that night was stormy to the point where the pastor and a few of the board members were battling about the direction for the congregation. Some board members did not see the need to have any special programmes or plans. Such members simply wanted to "attend church, have a good time and go back home." The pastor unfortunately did not win the battle that night nor for the next six (6) months.

Later, after reflecting on the situation in the congregation, the pastor backed off, and began visiting about two members per week, and engaging in the basic programmes of the church:

- **Sabbath school**
- **The mid-day Sabbath service**
- **The odd fortnightly prayer meeting**
- **The monthly board meeting.**

The pastor began focusing on and improving the spirituality of the congregation, using topics such as 'On the Run' (Series on the book of Jonah), and 'Afraid to Step Out'. The members continued to engage in 'run-of-the-mill' activities. Meanwhile, no outreach evangelistic work was done for that year.

Intervention & Strategy

During a scheduled pastoral visit to a family, the husband shared a gruesome and heart-breaking story. He shared that someone had used a demonic device in the church some twenty (20) years prior to us worshipping at this congregation. He further indicted that nothing had been done about it and it was still affecting some of the members. The shocking news forced the pastor to have a meeting with the two serving elders to verify the details.

Why hadn't the previous pastors not address this situation? Were they made aware of this 'cloud' which was still hanging over the congregation's 'head'? Why did the pastoral leaders take so long to address this serious spiritual issue? Did anyone notice that this congregation had not grown numerically nor spiritually for a long time? Who or what prevented the pastoral team from addressing this situation?

On meeting with the elders to verify the facts and discuss the situation, the pastor alerted the leaders that **there was a spiritual problem on hand and that spiritual problems require spiritual solutions.** Moreover, he informed them that the only spiritual solution to this problem was a rededication of the building. The elders unfortunately disagreed and resisted the idea. However, as the pastor persisted that this is the only spiritual solution, they acknowledged his perspective, after which he insisted that it needed to be brought to the Church Board.

The urgency of the situation forced the pastor to have the item as the primary item on the agenda. During the discussion , there was general disagreement with the idea of re-dedication. However, the pastor, being firm and determined about the spiritual progress of the congregation, alerted the board members of the need for the members to move forward spiritually and emotionally. Eventually, a date was set for the rededication early in the following year.

Impact of the Ministry

This special service, which was held in the second month, had a two-fold purpose: it succeeded in re-consecrating the building to the Lord and it was also a time for the members to re-commit themselves to God. Subsequent to this, there was energy and motivation in the congregation. We also observed that there was a renewed momentum, with leaders speaking positively and behaving more cooperatively. Of the ministry plans that were executed, there was a Community Guests' Day, the first in approximately sixty (60) years. By the end of the year, there was the first baptism in five (5) years in this congregation.

Furthermore, by the turn of the next year, the Board agreed to redecorate the sanctuary and also to acquire new furniture. One of the redecoration activities, was the removal of the old pulpit and using a lectern instead. The recommendation for the redecoration had to be discussed and agreed by the members. Such a meeting occurred on a Sunday evening early in the third year. The members who were present agreed to the new changes.

Within twenty-four (24) hours, on returning to the church to collect a few items, to his dismay, the pastor observed that the old wooden pulpit had already been ripped out and removed, with the space on the floor covered with the same colour carpet as the remainder of the sanctuary. Where did these members get the energy and motivation from to take down the old pulpit so quickly? Why were they so eager to start the redecoration? Emerging out of this, the members hosted an outreach programme which attracted contacts to the church from the community.

Conclusion

Spiritual and emotional issues tend to have a severe negative impact on congregations. Since the issue with demonic activities tear away the spirituality of a congregation, it appears that the lack of spiritual insight hindered the leaders' ability to address this issue previously. However, the work of every congregation is spiritual and needs spiritual resources to bring about the necessary results. Every congregation may have different degrees of ill-health, nevertheless, healing is important to any congregation if it is to carry out the Great Commission which Christ has left for every believer.

Case C: Well's Praise Centre

Background

Well's Praise Centre Church is located in a city of about 450 000 people, with the city situated on the outskirts of its rural geographical region. There were about forty (140) members during the time we worshipped at this congregation, however the number has reached some 210 members. Additionally, the majority of members are non-British . The members have been worshipping in their present building since the late 1960s. About a quarter of the membership is made up of youth (14 – 25+), half of the members are mature adults (26 – 50 + years) and the elderly (65 years +) make up the other quarter. The average age of the membership is 45 years old.

Intervention & Strategy

When we came to worship here, the congregation was embarking on a building project. Soon after, one of the members suddenly passed away and it shocked the entire congregation, the community and others around. This death left a hole in the congregation. However, as we approached the end of the year and prepared for our planning sessions, the Holy Spirit prompted us to focus on healing. In our planning sessions we shared thoughts. We set up the programme, with the theme being *A Journey Towards Total Wholeness,* focusing initially on forgiveness for the first month of the new year. In February, we focused on freedom and then used to last month of the Quarter to focus intently on prayer. This involved Days of Prayer and fasting, half night prayer services and a revival week.

In the second Quarter, we continued and focused on reconciliation and restoration. In an effort to be effective, we brought in resource individuals who were gifted in a ministry dealing with these topics. During the last two Quarters: July to December, we engaged in series preaching focusing on the Book of Mark, the Gospel which features many healing stories.

This approach was taken not because of the death, but we recognised that there have been residual issues (interpersonal, cultural, doctrinal etc) which were never resolved. Such issues began rising and affecting the congregation and the ministries, to the point that it became difficult to engage in ministry and achieve the mission of the church. Moreover, the pastor indicated that the distasteful environment, the general downturn in the congregation, the lack of support and co-operation and the behaviour of the leaders had instigated him to contemplate seriously on asking for a move away from the pastoral district.

Part of the intervention strategy was the use of the Holy Communion Service as a time of healing. The second Communion Service of the year took a different shape. From the outset, the pastor made the congregation aware of the new plan. He distributed slips of paper for **every person present and** informed them to **write out whatever issue(s) or person(s)** they are/have been struggling with up to the present time. The service took the following form:

Section 1

This involved a Short prayer a hymn, the weekly family prayer and the pastoral prayer. Prior to the pastoral prayer, the pastor alerted everyone to come forward with their slip of paper, tear it into pieces and drop it in the boxes which were placed at the foot of a cross at the altar. In Using writing therapy, the members were flushing themselves of these issues and giving them to the Lord. Afterwards, they were encouraged to remain at the altar where the pastor prayed for all of them. Then they were ushered immediately into the hall where they engaged in foot-washing.

Section 2

After we returned to the Sanctuary, the service resumed with a lively praise and worship session, collection of the offering, a sermonette and then the administering of the Holy Emblems. Out of this new format, the pastor sense immediately that the environment had changed and he gained a renewed desire to stay and work with the congregation.

Impact of the Ministry

The members expressed the general view that the topics have been beneficial to them personally and to the congregation. It was noticeable that most members attended many of the Sabbath services when these topics were presented. One of the benefits of the programme was God sustaining the congregation's finances inspite of the difficulties we had been experiencing. Moreover, we were able to conduct our yearly evangelistic outreach campaign, which brought the congregation together and more harmoniously. Out of this, we perceived that the congregation was ready to take off and engage in more evangelistic outreach work.

Conclusion

Although the issues were different, there was still a need for healing. From this we realised that conflicts and interpersonal issues hinders a congregation from engaging in the divine commission. The issues such as conflicts and a display of unco-operative attitude demanded that the emotional ill-health in the congregation be addressed urgently. Churches that are grappling with emotional and spiritual problems, along with other issues, need to address these issues through a programme such as holistic restoration.

PART E

Training Practicum, Titles & Tools

Come to Me, all *you* who labor and are heavy laden, and I will give you rest. [29] Take My yoke upon you and learn from Me, for I am gentle and lowly in heart, and you will find rest for your souls. [30] For My yoke *is* easy and My burden is light."

9
TRAINING COURSE PRACTICUM

HOLISTIC RESTORATION TRAINING COURSE PRACTICUM

Practicum 1

Deigh's Community Church is a young congregation with about 30 members, all from the African continent. The average age of the membership is 30 years old. It has had one pastor since it opened and used rented accommodation. Since its inception, it has had special programmes at least five times per quarter in the first three (3) years of its programme. Within its fourth year, some of the members began experiencing marital issues, which were highly cultural in nature. This affected the attendance of members and also the mission and ministry programmes of the congregation.

Soon after, a few families joined this congregation. But in less than six months, the new individuals expressed their disapproval with everything in the congregation: pastoral leadership, the attire of the female members, communion service, time for closing the premises etc. As time progressed there was severe conflict and immense tension, to the point that some of the former members began missing Sabbath services because the atmosphere was very tense and un-conducive for worship. Eventually, the congregation became split with there being two groups: the former members (except the leader who join the new attendees) versus the new attendees.

- As the leader of the implementation team for the Holistic Restoration programme, the Church Board has commissioned you to assist with the particular approach that would restore this congregation to good health. Design an intervention programme which you will share with the Pastor and the Board.

- With your team, diagnose the problem and suggest an appropriate approach (**e.g re-dedication, large group therapy/counselling, seminar & presentations on specific topics relating to the issues, stages in the hierarchy of holistic restoration, special Communion Service, intense spiritual programme, stewardship emphasis programmes etc**) that could bring healing to this congregation (**SEE APPENDIX B**).

- The plan should include assessing the readiness level of the congregation (**See SECTION 3**). Having shared the strategy with your pastor, report to the Board and share the direction you think would restore health to the congregation.

- Share the tools (*Emotionally Healthy Church Inventory etc*), resources (*Ministry of Healing,*) and materials that you would use to implement the programme (**SEE Section 11 & APPENDIX B).**

Practicum 2

Green Bay Church has about 145 members mainly of Afro-Caribbean descent. About just over half of the congregation are 50 years +. It has had three (3) pastors and three (3) interns in the last twelve (12) years. Some fifty years ago, a male member had children from two female members (one being his wife and another was a member). As time progressed, the children grew and matured, but have never interacted with each other. Even now that some of these children worship in the same congregation and are Board members, they do not interact, neither do they have a loving relationship. Other intimacy relationships between male and female members had occurred and had produced children.

Over the years, these issues were not resolved and have held back the congregation. Although the members mean well, it is evident there is ill-health in the congregation, in that the leaders see no need to move forward or to progress into new and innovative ministry.

Some time ago, a number of members brought a recommendation to set up a new congregation in another section of the town so that the evangelistic work can be widened. Many members disagreed with the idea since they wanted all the members to remain at the main church in an effort to assist financially with the building programme which has been at the planning stage for more than a decade.

Inspite of the disagreement, a team of members branched out, even though they did not have the mother church's blessing. Today, the establishment of this programme still creates a bitter taste in some members' mouth.

- As the leader of the implementation team, diagnose the situation based on the facts above. Share with the other team members what you think is the main issue and prayerfully recommend to the pastor and church board the most appropriate programme or combination of programmes that would address the problem and restore the congregation's health.

- Identify the resources, specific programmes and spiritual activities that could assist the members in progressing spiritually and emotionally.

Practicum 3

- Bracknest Church has gone through the year-long healing programme, *A Journey Towards Total Wholeness.* The congregation is on the verge of embarking on a major evangelistic programme. However, two months into the new year, some of the Board members (just over a quarter of the members are new to the Board for this year) have been plotting to 'bring down' the pastor. There have been verbal arguments on the board, some individuals refuse to attend meetings and some leaders have not reported to the Board about their programmes. Furthermore, the finances of this local church are very poor to the point where it is unable to pay its monthly bills (utility, loans etc). Moreover, there is very little money, if any, to conduct ministry.

- Having been assigned the responsibility of being leader of the implementation team, suggest a follow-up approach which would assist the congregation in experiencing a greater degree of health.

- In your planning, diagnose the situation, state the length of the programme, and identify potential resource persons to facilitate the presentations or preach the sermonic messages.

Practicum 4

The Loughs Church is located in a mega city and has about 320 members, with half from the African continent and the other half are of Afro-Caribbean descent. It has had five (5) pastors and three (3) interns in the last twelve years. About three-quarters of the congregation are in the 30 – 50 age group, with the average age of the membership being 45 years.

Over the last few months, there have been major conflicts over the behaviour of members of the pastoral team. The issue has spilled into the congregation, with some members supporting one group of pastoral leaders and another group giving support to the other side. Moreover, the support has been split along ethnic lines.

Inspite of various meetings to resolve the issue, no progress has been made. Actually, there is now sharp tension and severe conflicts in the congregation, with these two major ethnic groups battling with each other. Unfortunately, the pastor is caught in the middle of the conflict and finds it difficult to address the problem.

- As the leader of the implementation team, the pastor has asked you to assist him in preparing the church for the year-long programme, entitled *A Journey Towards Total Wholeness.* He has asked you to share some ideas for the first Quarter.

- Using the outline below, prepare a plan of how you would go about your task in the first month. In your planning, consider the need for a 10-day prayer and fasting programme (**SEE APPENDIX A**)

OUTLINE PLAN

*NB. For each **Month,** there is a different theme (see the topics in bold italics).*

1st QUARTER

1st Month: *Forgiveness*: **1)** Focusing on sub-themes of (a) forgiving yourself; b)forgiving each other (c) receiving forgiveness from God.

2) Studying topics such as (a) The Role of the Holy Spirit in Spiritual Revival of the congregation (b) The Role of the Holy Spirit in the Life of the congregation (c) Parables of the Kingdom-The Unforgiving Servant (d) Parables of the Kingdom-The Unjust Steward

3) Hosting monthly Day of Prayer & Fasting.

2nd Month: Freedom: (1) Addressing (a) Emotional Freedom, (b) Spiritual Freedom through sermons and presentations

(2) Studying topics such as (a) Parables of the Kingdom-The Unforgiving Servant (d) Parables of the Kingdom-The Unjust Steward

(3) Hosting monthly Day of Prayer & Fasting.

3rd Month: Discipleship & Prayer *(1)* Teaching topics such as (a) 'The Active God in the Congregation (Acts 4); (b) 'The Power of Intercessory Prayer'

(2) Studying topics such as (a) The Role of the Holy Spirit in Prayer & Personal Devotions; (b) Developing a Personal Relationship with God (c) How to Maintain a Personal Relationship with God

(3) Quarterly Day of Prayer & Fasting

(4) Special Communion Service Focusing on the Theme of : **On Death Row**: Sub-theme—*Give Me Another Chance*

Practicum 5

The Hillings Community Church has about 80 members on the books, but about 50 are actively worshipping weekly. Most of the members are in the 30-45 age group, with the average age being 45. The congregation is made up mainly of three (3) families, all of who have leading positions. Of all the members, only one family lives outside the immediate church community. This congregation has had five (5) pastors in the last twelve (12) years. Prior to the year 2000, some 120 members have left this congregation over a ten-year period. Moreover, inspite of the evangelistic campaigns that have been conducted, the new members that have been baptised tend to spend no more than two (2) years in this congregation and then become inactive.

During the 1970s, and 1980s, it was alleged that the head deacon was involved in homosexual activities. Nevertheless, he continued to serve in the same role until the year 2000, when he died. However, no facts have ever been established, hence the matter was never addressed. Furthermore, there have been a number of conflicts between members and also between families. Efforts have been made to address the underlying issue, however the conflicts continue to occur.

- As the leader of the implementation team, plan a 10-day special prayer and fasting programme which would prepare this congregation for the holistic restoration ministry. In preparing your plan, consider the resources you would need (**personnel, speakers, materials, tools etc).**

- Identify the necessary tools and resources you would use to prepare the congregation to become healthy again. In your planning also, identify which approach (**Special Communion, re-dedication etc)** or combination of approaches would be effective in restoring health to this congregation.

Practicum 6

Your pastor has been assigned to your 85-member church just over a year ago. You are a leader in this youthful congregation, which has about five (5) special programmes per quarter. During his routine pastoral visits, all the members have been sharing the same sentiments: " Our congregation has problems. People are not speaking to each other. People are not working together. You need to do something about this." He has also noticed that many visitors do not attend the weekly worship services, neither do many members bring visitors to special programmes.

On inquiring about this strange phenomenon, the pastor was told: "It was not always like this. We usually have about 100 individuals here on most Sabbaths." Furthermore, about half of the congregation has refused to serve in various ministry capacities, thus putting a strain on the other willing members. The pastor supports the perspective that the weekly attendance at the Sabbath Service should be higher than the membership of the congregation. However, the opposite exists in this congregation.

- The pastor has approached you as a leader in this congregation and asked you to share your insights. What is the issue? Is this congregation unhealthy? How would you assist in restoring the health?

- Prayerfully, prepare a strategy to assist the pastor in ministering to the needs of this congregation.

10
RESTORATION SEMINARS & CONFERENCE TITLES

SERIES 1:   Part A – Impacting the Congregation With Spiritual Care

Presentation #1: Congregational Spirituality: It's A Heart Matter
Presentation #2: Special Measures for the Congregation
Presentation #3: Worship: Experiencing the Power of God's presence
Presentation #4: Spiritual Ill-Health And Paralysis: The Common Link

Part B – Experiencing the Power of Spiritual Care

Presentation # 1: Relief From Your Painful Past
Presentation # 2: Unshackled – **Part I**
Presentation # 3: Unshackled – **Part II**
Presentation # 4: Tears of the Innocent Speak Loudly

** ** ** **

SERIES 2:   Part A: The Balm in Gilead – Preparation Process

Presentation #1: Uncovering the Layers of Your Painful Past
Presentation #2:Escaping the Roadside of Life
Presentation #3:Weapons of Mass Destruction
Presentation #4:The Power Struggle: Comfort, Fear or Hope

Part B: Paving the Path Towards Restoration

Presentation #1: Opening the Hurting Heart
Presentation #2: Preparing the Heart for Restoration
Presentation #3: The Wounded Heart at the Feet of Jesus
Presentation #4: Forgiveness, Peace and Restoration: The Common Link

** ** ** **

SERIES 3:   The Balm in Gilead – An Intervention Strategy

Presentation #1: The Healing Power of Forgiveness
Presentation #2: A Journey Towards Total Freedom

Presentation #3: Escaping Your Pit Without Being Angry
Presentation #4: A Journey Towards Reconciliation: Building Broken Bridges

SERIES 4:   Maintaining Hope in Adversity

Presentation #1: Living with Threats from the Enemy
Presentation #2:On the Run—Responding to the Enemy's Threats
Presentation #3:Preparing for a Journey of Restoration
Presentation #4: Being Re-positioned on Your Journey

**   **   **   **

SERIES 5:   Part A: Refuge for the Emotionally Wounded

Presentation #1: Relief for a Burdened Heart
Presentation #2:Locating the Rock in Your 'Desert'
Presentation #3: Living Under Divine Shelter
Presentation #4:Assurance of Divine Protection

Part B: The Balm for the Emotional Wounds

Presentation #1: God-given Beauty for Human Ashes
Presentation #2: The Power in the Oil of Joy
Presentation #3: Impact of the Garment of Praise
Presentation #4: Wearing the Garments of Salvation

**   **   **   **

Series 6: The Healing Power of a Compassionate Heart

Presentation #1: Our Deeds Have Come Before the Light
Presentation #2: The Human Heart: A Battle with and Response to Sin
Presentation #3: Will You Stone the Condemned?
Presentation #4: Healing the Condemned

_____Training Workshop Titles

**Level I:
Assessing the Emotional
& Spiritual Health of
a Congregation**

- Assessing Restoration Readiness & Preparing the Path Towards Restoration
- Understanding Congregational
- Dynamics I
- Uncovering the Layers of Your Past
- Experiencing the Healing Power of Forgiveness
- Genogram Your Family/Church
- Implementing the Emotionally Healthy Church Inventory
- Diagnosing the Problem
- PRACTICUM **I**

**Level II:
Preparing the Congregation
for Holistic Restoration**

- Implementing a Ministry of Holistic Restoration (**PART I**)
- Phases of Holistic Restoration
- Understanding Congregational
- Dynamics **II**
- A Journey Towards Total Freedom
- Escaping Your Pit Without Anger
- Analysing A congregation's Life Cycle
- PRACTICUM **II**
- And more

**Level III:
Experiencing
Holistic Restoration**

- Designing Intervention Programmes
- Implementing a Ministry of Holistic Restoration (**PART II**)
- Applying A Hierarchy of Holistic Restoration
- God-given Beauty for Human Ashes
- Re-Building Broken Bridges
- PRACTICUM **III**
- And more

Pre-Assessment Holistic Restoration Questionnaire

Dear Brethren,

The Leaders of your congregation have recognised the need to request for a series of Restoration seminars and a workshop to be conducted. However, in order to gain an insight into the overall perspective of the congregation's needs, I would be grateful if you could complete the below questionnaire and return it to me as soon as you can.

Please note that you **DO NOT NEED** to write your name on the questionnaire, since the details and views will be treated with confidentiality.

Thank you very much for your assistance in allowing me to gather this information so that I can better serve your congregation.

ADMINISTRATION PROCEDURE:

1) Please give to each Board member to complete. (2) Additionally, for small Boards with less than twenty-five members, give to ten (10) members who are very active in the congregation. **OR** For medium Boards (25-40 members), give to all Board members and 10 active lay members. **OR** For large Boards (40 + members), give to all Board members and 20 active lay members.

CONGREGATIONAL DATA

Please fill in the information below as best as you can

Name of Church ....

Membership (Total on Books)...members

Total Active Membership (Those who attend weekly services)................................members

PERSONAL DATA

Please tick/circle the item which refers to you

1. I am (a) member of the pastoral team (b) a departmental leader (c) a regular member

2. Gender: Male ( ) Female ( )

3. How long have you been worshipping at your congregation?

    (a) 0 – 5 years (   )   (b) 6 – 10 years (   )   (c) 11 – 15 years   (d) 16 – 20 years

    (e) 20 + years (   )

QUESTIONNAIRE

Scale:

Strongly Agreed – 5   Agreed – 4   Uncertain – 3   Disagree – 2   Strongly Disagree – 1

No.	ITEMS	SA	A	U	D	SD
	A. Empowering leadership					
1	I always accept and respond to suggestions from members of the pastoral team (elders and pastors).					
2	The decisions and plans which the pastoral team share with the other leaders are not in the best interest of the overall development of the congregation.					
3	The pastoral team delegates responsibilities to other members of the congregation					
4	Our pastoral team arranges and provides training programmes for other lay leaders					
5	The pastoral team in our congregation encourages lay members to undertake training and sponsors them					
6	We support and respond to the pastor's leadership without any reservations					

No.	ITEMS	SA	A	U	D	SD
	B. Gift-based ministry					
7	Members of our congregation engage in areas of ministry according to their gifts and the area for which they have a passion					
8	Various events and programmes occur in my congregation, but there do not highlight ministry based on spiritual gifts.					
	C. Passionate spirituality					
9	Individual and corporate prayer are key elements in the life of our congregation					
10	Most of the members attend the structured bible studies, prayer services; and prayer and fasting sessions					
11	The leaders have set up a mentoring and discipleship programme to nurture new members					
12	The members support social activities more than evangelistic programmes					
	D. Effective structures					
13	Our pastoral team and lay leaders meet to create and provide the mission and the vision for the congregation					
14	The members do not know who to contact when there is a problem but take matters into their own hands					
15	The congregation's administration is very poor in managing the programmes and finances					
	E. Inspiring worship services					
16	I sense the presence of God during our worship sessions and enjoy worshipping in this congregation					
17	The worship sessions focus on show, self and performance					
18	The worship sessions are disorganised and unplanned					
	F. Holistic small groups					
19	Members of our congregation are very eager to become involved in holistic small group ministry					
20	Our pastoral team members passionately promote and support the setting up of holistic small group ministry					

No.	ITEMS	SA	A	U	D	SD
21	Holistic small group ministry is part of my congregation's strategy for nurture and evangelism					
	G. Need-orientated evangelism					
22	The ministries and programmes in my congregation are planned with the view of reaching out to the community					
23	I do not see the need to be involved in a ministry which impact the neighbourhood					
24	Over the last year, new ministries and programmes have been developed to meet the needs of the community around our congregation					
25	Our congregation has a negative image in the community and does not attract neighbours to its services					
	H. Loving relationships					
26	I know where at least twenty (20) of the members of this congregation live					
27	The members of the pastoral team co-operate with and support each other					
28	The environment in our congregation is negative and does not entice me to interact with the other members					
29	Visitors are generally not welcomed with a gift to the church					
30	Leaders and Members do not resolve problems quickly and they are left without being solved for a long time					

APPENDICES

APPENDIX A

10 DAYS

OF

PRAYER with FASTING

PASTORAL DISTRICT OF ....CHURCH

Preamble

The year has rushed upon us and is swiftly moving ahead into eternity, while there are many individuals who are still bound by satanic forces, evil and vice. This reminds me of that striking admission that the Prophet Jeremiah declared: The harvest is past, the summer has ended, and we are not saved" (Jer 8:20). How then can we reach the unsaved? But how can we evangelise if our congregation is experiencing ill-health? How can the communities around us be impacted upon? What do we need, as Christ's disciples, to go into all the world and preach the Gospel? We are aware that "Near the close of earth's harvest, a special bestowal of spiritual grace is promised to prepare the church for the coming of the Son of man. This outpouring of the Spirit is likened to the falling of the latter rain; and it is for this added power that Christians are to send their petitions to the Lord of the harvest . . . ."[48] More importantly, Scripture reminds that "the Lord shall make bright clouds, and give them showers of rain. He will cause to come down . . . the rain, the former rain, and the latter rain," (Zechariah 10:1; Joel 2:23).

Such an infilling of the power of the Holy Ghost can only occur when we reach out to the Source of healing power, the Almighty God. With this being the case, I implore you to sense the urgency for times of reflection and prayer in your lives and in the local congregation. Moreover, as you use this district—(congregation-) wide prayer initiative to intercede with and for each other during the next ten (10) days, may you truly experience a revival in your personal lives and in the life of your congregations.

Additionally, when we look through our cities and towns we are faced with various communities which must be reached with the Everlasting Gospel. I would like to encourage you to make the sacrifice for these ten nights. More importantly, whenever you covenant to meet with God in prayer, you can guarantee that you will experience His power in your lives. In fact, it is the power of God that energises us, keeps us focused and empowers us to carry out the Master's Great Commission as we seek the lost in our communities.

Furthermore, this is an awesome and poignant time in the history of your district/congregation since you are about to embark on a *journey towards total wholeness,* which is facilitated through the **Ministry of Holistic Restoration.** I encourage you to seek for the divine intervention which will restore your congregation to emotional and spiritual health so that you can rise up and engage in the Master's work in the communities around. I long for you to experience the tremendous blessings that this time of earnest prayer promises to provide.

Yours in the Master's Service
Victor D Marshall (Programme Co-ordinator)

10 DAYS

OF

PRAYER with FASTING

Below is a suggested format for the **one-hour** service:

- Opening Prayer/
- Praise & Worship Session
- Personal Time / Group Prayer Session **I**
- The Word (**15-minute Message)**
- Personal Prayer Time/Group Prayer Session **II**
- Thanksgiving & Praise through Song

SUGGESTED DAILY FOCUS

DAY 1

Wednesday, January 04

FOCUS TEXT: Psalm 32:5 (AMP)

"Iacknowledged my sin to You, and my iniquity I did not hide. I said, I will confess my transgressions to the Lord [continually unfolding the past till all is told]—then You [instantly] forgave me the guilt and iniquity of my sin. Selah [pause, and calmly think of that]!"

PRAYER FOCUS: 1) Forgiveness of sins, cleansing of our soul and personal preparation for ministry; **2)** In-filling of the Holy Spirit for mission

DAY 2

Thursday, January 05

FOCUS TEXT: Galatians 6:1-2 (NIV)

"Brothers, if someone is caught in a sin, you who are spiritual should restore him gently. But watch yourself, or you also may be tempted. Carry each other's burdens, and in this way you will fulfil the law of Christ."

PRAYER FOCUS: 1) Personal revival for you and your prayer partners and divine direction for your lives
2) Spiritual growth and personal needs of your prayer partner

DAY 3

Friday, January 06

FOCUS TEXT: Psalm 51:5-12
Seek God

. . . for **spiritual motivation and a renewed heart** to serve Him and be committed to His Work.

"Purify me with hyssop, and I shall be clean [ceremonially]; wash me, and I shall [in reality] be whiter than snow" (Psalm 51:7, AMP).

SUGGESTED DAILY FOCUS

DAY 4

Sabbath, January 07,

FOCUS TEXT: 1 Thess 5:9-11 (NKJV)

"For God did not appoint us to wrath, but to obtain salvation through our Lord Jesus Christ, who died for us, that whether we wake or sleep, we should live together with Him. Therefore comfort each other and edify one another, just as you also are doing."

PRAYER FOCUS: 1) Intercede for our church members and regular attendees to experience a spiritual revival
2) Spiritual eagerness to follow Jesus in the Christian journey.

DAY 5

Sunday, January 08

FOCUS TEXT: Proverbs 3:5-8
Seek God

. . . for **divine direction in your personal life and for your family/relatives.**

"Trust in the LORD with all your heart and lean not on your own understanding; in all your ways acknowledge him, and he will make your paths straight" (Prov 3:5-6, NIV).

SUGGESTED DAILY FOCUS

DAY 6

Monday, January 09

FOCUS TEXT: Prov 3:3-6 (KJV)

³Let not mercy and truth forsake thee: bind them about thy neck; write them upon the table of thine heart: ⁴So shalt thou find favour and good understanding in the sight of God and man. ⁵Trust in the LORD with all thine heart; and lean not unto thine own understanding. ⁶In all thy ways acknowledge him, and he shall direct thy paths.

PRAYER FOCUS: 1) For a spirit of unity and co-operation among members and leaders
              2) For spiritual issues in the congregation (unfaithfulness in tithing etc)

DAY 7

Tuesday, January 10

FOCUS TEXT: Mt 10:6-8 (KJV)

"But go rather to the lost sheep of the house of Israel. ⁷And as ye go, preach, saying, The kingdom of heaven is at hand. Heal the sick, cleanse the lepers, raise the dead, cast out devils: freely ye have received, freely give."

PRAYER FOCUS: 1) For the spirit of forgiveness to prevail among the members; forgiveness of sins among members.
              2) Spiritual awakening in the congregation
              3) Pray for the condition of the congregation (openness, honesty, hearts of humility)

SUGGESTED DAILY FOCUS

Wednesday, January 11,
(SPECIAL DAY OF PRAY & FAST—11 am – 3 pm)

FOCUS TEXT: Nehemiah 1:6-7 (NIV)

"Let your ear be attentive and your eyes open to hear the prayer your servant is praying before you day and night for your servants, the people of Israel. I confess the sins we Israelites, including myself and my father's house, have committed against you. We have acted very wickedly towards you. We have not obeyed the commands, decrees and laws you gave your servant Moses"

PRAYER FOCUS: 1) Intercede for the leaders that they would surrender to God's leading;
2) Plead for the barriers to good health in the congregation to be removed;
3) Restoration of relationships in the congregation

DAY 8

Thursday, January 12,

FOCUS TEXT: Luke 10: 2-3 (KJV)

"A new command I give you: Love one another. As I have loved you, so you must love one another. By this all men will know that you are my disciples, if you love one another.

PRAYER FOCUS: 1) Emotional and interpersonal issues in the congregation;
2) Your personal relationship with other members

SUGGESTED DAILY FOCUS

DAY 9

Friday, January 13,

FOCUS TEXT: Mt 11:28-30

Come to me, all you who are weary and burdened, and I will give you rest. Take my yoke upon you and learn from me, for I am gentle and humble in heart, and you will find rest for your souls.For my yoke is easy and my burden is light.

PRAYER FOCUS: 1)   Recommitment of members to God; Re-dedication of their lives;
                       2)   Family relationships in the congregations

DAY 10

Sabbath, January 14,

FOCUS TEXT: John 16:13 (NIV)

But when he, the Spirit of truth, comes, he will guide you into all truth. He will not speak on his own; he will speak only what he hears, and he will tell you what is yet to come.

PRAYER FOCUS: 1)   Intercede for the Holy Spirit to dwell among the members
                       2)   Pray for our inactive members who no longer worship or follow the Lord;
                       3)   Plead for a changed and spiritually conducive environment in the congregation.

Conclusion

The 10 days of Prayer with fasting is an opportunity for us to be renewed and experience God's faithfulness to prayer. "Those only who are constantly receiving fresh supplies of grace, will have power proportionate to their daily need and their ability to use that power. Instead of looking forward to some future time when, through a special endowment of spiritual power, they will receive a miraculous fitting up for soul winning, they are yielding themselves daily to God, that He may make them vessels meet for His use. Daily they are improving the opportunities for service that lie within their reach. Daily they are witnessing for the Master wherever they may be, whether in some humble sphere of labor in the home, or in a public field of usefulness".[49]

Having embarked on these ten days of searching and weeping for Divine intervention, may you press forward with courage to assist your congregation in experiencing the healing power of God. These ten days have sought to lead individuals and congregations into a time of seeking for and extending forgiveness, addressing interpersonal issues and paving the way for reconciliation and restoration of relationships. By engaging in spiritual disciplines such as prayer and fasting, it is hoped that participants experienced some degree of transformation in their emotional health and spiritual maturity. I pray that you will be able to share with someone the impact which you have witnessed from this experience.

OUTLINE PLAN FOR
IMPLEMENTING THE MINISTRY OF HOLISTIC RESTORATION

*NB. For each **Month**, there is a different theme (see the topics in bold italics).*

2nd QUARTER PROGRAMME

1st Month: *Reconciliation*:

    1) Focusing on sub-themes of (a) reconciling to yourself; b) reconciling to each other (c) reconciling to God.

    2) Studying topics such as (a) Reconciliation: The Preparation Process;
(b) Relationship between repentance, confession and reconciliation.

    3) Hosting monthly Day of Prayer & Fasting.

2nd Month: *Restoration*:

    (1) Addressing (a) Emotional Restoration, (b) Spiritual Restoration through sermons and presentations

    (2) Studying topics such as (a) Processes of humility and forgiveness in
Spiritual Restoration (b) The Link Between Spiritual Restoration and healing.

    (3) Hosting monthly Day of Prayer & Fasting.

3rd Month: *Fellowship*

    1) Family Fellowship Day;

    2) Quarterly Day of Prayer & Fasting

    3) Special Communion Service: Sub-theme—*Bearing His Cross*

3rd QUARTER PROGRAMME

Series Preaching: Preaching from the Gospel of Mark which focuses mainly on healing. Since some of the chapters have common links or similar material/ topics, two consecutive chapters can be grouped together and be used as the major text from which to draw a small portion for the sermon.

1st Month: Studying aspects of Prayer; Monthly Prayer & Fasting Service

2ⁿᵈ Month: 1) Study Topic: End Time Events such as

        (a) How to respond to the existence of The Wheat with the Tares

        (b) The Shaking

        (c) The Early Tme of Trouble

    2) Monthly Prayer & Fasting Service;

    3) Week of Revival & Stewardship Emphasis

3ʳᵈ Month: Study Topics—Second Coming of Christ;

    Quarterly Day of Prayer & Fasting;

    Special Communion Service—Sub-Theme : Forsaken at the Cross.

4th QUARTER PROGRAMME

Series Preaching: Preaching from the Gospel of Mark Continued

1ˢᵗ Month: 1) Studying topics such as Revival & Reformation through Prayer;

        Revival & Reformation: Worshipping with a True Heart

    2) Quarterly Day of Prayer & Fasting

2ⁿᵈ Month: 1) Studying topics such as Experiencing Daily Sanctification as part of Salvation

    2) Special Communion Service—Sub-Theme: *Crucified*

NB: The above themes emerge from the stages of holistic restoration. During each month, it would be important to alert the preacher of the theme and sub-theme so that he/she can prepare the message strategically. The topics to be studied are used on Wednesday evening during the prayer meetings, while the Quarterly Days of Prayer and fasting can be held on Sabbaths.

BIBLIOGRAPHY

1 Peter L. Scazzero and Warren Bird , *The Emotionally Healthy Church: A Strategy for Discipleship That Actually Changes Lives,* Updated and Expanded Edition (Grand Rapids, MI: Zondervan Publishing House, 2010), p.10.

2 Ellen G. White, *Testimonies for the Church*, Vol 7 (Mountain View, CA: Pacific Press Publishing Association, 1902), *p 59.*

3 Scazzero, *The Emotionally Healthy Church,* p.20.

4 Ellen G. White, *The Ministry of Healing* Mountain View, California: Pacific Press,1942), p.7.

5 Joel B. Green, "Healing" in T. D. Alexander, Brian S. Rosner, (eds), *New Dictionary of Biblical Theology* (Leicester, UK: Inter-Varsity Press, 2000), pp. 536-540 (537).

6 Green, "Healing", p.538.

7 Robert H. Grundy, *Mark: A Commentary on His Apology for the Cross,*(Grand Rapids, MI: Eerdman, 1993), p.268.

8 Green, "Healing", p.539.

9 Green, "Healing", p.537.

10 Donald H. Juel, *The Gospel of Mark* (Nashville, TN Abingdon Press, 1999), p.115;Bonnie, B. Thurston, *Preaching Mark* (Minneapolis: Fortress Press, 2002), p. 27.

11 Additional Old Testament references can be found in Deuteronomy 7:15; 32:39; Psalms 6:2-3;30:2;41:4;103:3;147:3;Isaiah 30:26; 53:5 and 1 Peter 2:24.

12 Jesus' ministry made Him famous among Galileans and people from many other geographical areas. See Mt. 4:24-25.

13 Tom Shepherd, "Your Faith Has Saved You: A Theology of Health and Healing in the Canonical Gospels" in James W. Zackrison, (Ed),*The Master's Healing Touch* (Hagerston, MD: Review & Herald, 1997), pp. 49-58 (49-50).

14 Shepherd, pp. 50-51.

15 Craig A. Evans "Mark", in *Commentary on the Bible* , Ed. James D. G. Dunn and John W. Rogerson, (Michigan: Eerdmans, 2003), p. 1079.

16 In Acts 19:11-12, the Apostle Paul engaged in a method similar to that described in Acts 5:12-16, in that aprons and handkerchiefs which were put on Paul's body, were used to heal the sick.

17 Candida R. Moss, "The Man With the Flow of Power: Porous Bodies in Mark 5:25-34" In Journal of Biblical Literature, 2010, Vol 129 (3), pp. 507–519 (509-510.

18 Green, "Healing", p.536.

19 Green, "Healing", p.537.

20 Ibid.

21 White, *The Ministry of Healing* , p.8.

22 White, *The Ministry of Healing* , p.143.

23 Ellen G. White, *Counsels on Health* (Mountain View, California: Pacific Press,1923), p.31.

24 White, *The Ministry of Healing* , p.111.

25 White, *The Ministry of Healing* , p.112

26 Ellen G. White, *Welfare Ministry* (Mountain View, California: Pacific Press,1952), p.71.

27 White, *The Ministry of Healing* , p.152.

28 Ellen G. White *Testimonies for the Church,* Vol 9 (Mountain View, CA: Pacific Press Publishing Association, 1909), *p. 42.*

29 Ellen G. White *Testimonies for the Church,* Vol 6 (Mountain View, CA: Pacific Press Publishing Association, 1948), *pp. 296-297.*

30 White, *Testimonies for the Church,* Vol 6, *p. 435.*

31 White, *Testimonies for the Church,* Vol 7, *pp.18-19.*

32 Ellen G. White used a pejorative term which is outdated globally since there have been great advancements in addressing inequalities among people with disabilities. Hence, I have replaced the word with a more inclusive and non-discriminatory term in Italics.

33 White, *Counsels on Health,* p.28

34 White, *Testimonies for the Church,* Vol 6, *p. 426.*

35 Ellen G. White, *Christian Service* (Mountain View, CA: Pacific Press Publishing Association, 1925), *p. 107.*

36 White, *Christian Service, p. 41.*

37 Ellen G. White, *Testimonies for the Church,* Vol 8 (Mountain View, CA: Pacific Press Publishing Association, 1958), *p 251.*

38 Ellen G. White, *Acts of the Apostles* (Mountain View, CA: Pacific Press, 1941), p.11.

39 Dennis Greenberg and Christine A. Padesky, *Mind Over Mood: Change How You Feel by Changing the Way You Think* (New York: The Guildford Press, 1995), p.16

40 Greenberg and Padesky, *Mind Over Mood,* p. 21.*:*

41 White, *Acts of the Apostles*, p.9.

42 Ellen G. White, *Testimonies for the Church,* Vol 3 (Mountain View, CA: Pacific Press Publishing Association, 4ᵗʰ edn, 1948), *p 228*

43 R. Clifford Jones, "The Pastor as a Visionary" in S. D. Cassimy, A. J. Jules & N. Satelmajer (Eds), *A Guide to Effective Pastoral Ministry* (Nampa, Idaho: Pacific Press Publishing Association, 2009), p. 39.

44 Jones, "The Pastor as a Visionary", p.40. Italics Added.

45 White, *The Ministry of Healing,* p. 241.

46 White, Desire of Ages, p.240.

47 White in *Testimonies to Ministers,* p.354

48 White, *Acts of the Apostles,* p.55.

49 White, *Acts of the Apostles,* p.55.